Conversations with Oprah Donald Trump & Jesus

Marion TD Lewis

Conversations with Oprah Donald Trump & Jesus

Marion TD Lewis
Waterfall Press

Copyright © 2008, 2015 by M. Lewis. All Rights reserved.
Published by Waterfall Press, Inc. New York, New York
No part of this publication may be reproduced, stored in a retrieval system, or transmitted in any form or by any means, electronic, mechanical, photocopying, recording, scanning, or otherwise, except as permitted under Section 107 or 108 of the 1976 United States Copyright Act, without either prior written permission of the Publisher, or authorization through payment of the appropriate per copy fee to the Copyright Clearance Center, Inc. 222 Rosewood Drive, Danvers MA 01923, (978) 750-8400 fax (978) 646-8600, or on the web at www.copyright.com Requests to the Publisher for permission should be addressed to contact@englishlanguageglobal.com
Limit of Liability/Disclaimer of Warranty: While the publisher and author have used their best efforts in preparing this book, they make no representations or warranties with respect to the accuracy or completeness of the contents of this book and specifically disclaim any implied warranties of merchantability or fitness for a particular purpose. NO warranty may be created or extended by sales representatives or written sales materials. The advice and strategies contained herein may not be suitable for your situation. The publisher is not engaged in rendering professional services, and you should consult with a professional where appropriate.

Any slights against people or organizations are unintentional.

Library of Congress Cataloguing in Publication Data:
Lewis, M.
2nd Edition
Conversations with Oprah Donald Trump and Jesus
ISBN: 9780966389333
1. Self Improvement, Personal.   2. Success   3.Celebrity   4 Donald Trump   5 Oprah Winfrey

Printed in the United States of America
10 9 8 7 6 5 4 3 2 1

Conversations with Oprah Donald Trump & Jesus

To my parents,
and to bach and ben

Acknowledgments

I thank God for giving me the inspiration to write this book. I thank my parents for their never-ending support, patience and unconditional love. My sister Monica deserves a huge thank you for her editorial assistance with this book and her trooper attitude with all the other projects I have taken on in recent years. Monica, you really were the wind beneath my wings so many times. You were able to provide such clarity for me on numerous occasions when I felt I had certainly lost my way. I love you so much and I want you to know that I've got your back. I will always have your back. I thank the editors, typesetters and printers at Lulu.com for doing such a marvelous job. I thank my friend Julie for reading the manuscript and giving me feedback. I also thank my friend Sam Musora for his life-long support, and specifically for his assistance with this project.

Nobody makes me laugh more than Sam Musora; I am blessed to have met this human being and to have him in my life. He is a gift to me from God. I thank my friend Michael Ryan for reading the manuscript and telling me his thoughts. He's a very busy man now being that he's Vice President of an investment concern in Midtown Manhattan. So I am privileged to have had his assistance with this. Thanks to the rest of the Lewis clan: Bridget, Angela, Johan, Charlene, Jennifer, Shika, Jawaan, Stefan, William, Henry, Jono, Nicholas, Zachary, Jazmin, Ariel, and Matthew. All my love and appreciation to each and every one of you. Finally, thanks to my cats, Bachanalia and Benjamin. I just would have lost my mind a long time ago without those two. Oh, and thanks to Stanley Shapiro because it was following a seemingly mundane conversation with him that it occurred to me that it was time to write another book.

Contents

Acknowledgments

Introduction

Note to reader

First set of vignettes—Think Big

One: A Private Jet

Two: The heavy-hitter mind-set

Three: God is rich (and you can be too)

Four: Expand to infinity

Five: Carrie's Manolo Blaniks were not a type of 401K

Six: Watch the pennies (and put notes in a jar)

Second set of vignettes—Put away childish things

Seven: Mistakes are teachable moments

Eight: Childish Things must be put away

Nine: Write it down!

Ten: Embrace the itch

Eleven: Stop apologizing; it's their fault not yours

Twelve: Ye are mortal

Thirteen: Who cares what anybody else is doing?

Fourteen: Worry about yourself yet give a fig about what is going on in the world because it's right

Third set of vignettes—No Frogs Please

Fifteen: Infatuation is folly

Sixteen: Be thankful for your vajayjay (or whatever you have)

Seventeen: Don't settle for a frog

Eighteen: The Breast Lift (to do it or not to do it?)

Nineteen: Cellulite, Grey Hairs, Chin Hairs

Twenty: Slay the "Mongoose"

Fourth set of vignettes—Find your own comfort zone

Twenty-one: How to choose a friend

Twenty-two: Frenemies

Twenty-three: Who do you dress for?

Twenty-four: Wear comfortable Jimmy Choos (but buy a condo first)

Twenty-five: Mud Baths

Fifth set of vignettes—Life is just a rubrics cube

Twenty-six: A good doc is hard to find

Twenty-seven: Good health is worth more than a billion dollars

Twenty-eight—Quit a job that gives you angst (but don't go bankrupt)

Twenty-nine—Make up your mind!

Thirty—Ask, but don't nag

Thirty-one—Even rich people have problems (behold Jennifer Anniston)

Thirty-two—Life is just a rubrics cube

Thirty-three—Pessimism as a motivator

Thirty-four—Let them see you cry

Sixth set of vignettes—Paris, Everest, Joy and Cake

Thirty-five—A trip to Paris

Thirty-six—Find your Everest and climb it

Thirty-seven—The herd can be wrong

Thirty-eight—Destroy the Weakling to get to the lion

Thirty-nine—Your joy is your job

Forty—Eat your cake and have it too (don't be bulimic)

To sum up

Appendix, Bibliography, Glossary & Index

Introduction

People keep telling me that 40 is the new 25 but all I can think is I am half way through my life (assuming I live to be eighty) and I feel like the perfect candidate for an episode of the Oprah Winfrey Show: Makeover Your Life after the big 40! How to fix your Big Mess! The world's quintessential late bloomer, turning forty feels to me like getting hit by a mid-life tsunami. A nervous breakdown right about now is tempting, but unfortunately there's no time for such a luxurious indulgence. I've already lost a decade while I was busy being the oldest adolescent in the Western Hemisphere; there's a lot of lost ground for me to make up. Am I the only forty year old who feels like this, I wonder?

What isn't wrong with my life? My career is hardly moving momentously. I am still single and have been since circa Ollie North was busted for the Iran Contra affair (well, almost.) I can't proudly say "I'm divorced" like normal people my age because I have never married. While my baby sisters are popping out babies a mile a minute, I have no kids. And let's not even talk about how long it's been since I actually engaged in activity that could even accidentally result in the production of kids.

I have no house in the suburbs or SUV. Please, I still don't even have a driver's license even though it's been on my list of things to do for the past twenty five years!

My bank account balances are miniscule; I'm so broke that, at this juncture, I can't buy myself one lousy pair of black patent leather Jimmy Choo pumps unless I charge it on my credit card.

How come there are so many people with hundreds of pairs of Jimmy Choo pumps and I can't even afford one pair? That's not all. I do not own any real estate. I am shoulder deep in educational debt. My Fico Score is only fair (and it's been worse!)

To top it all off, I've had to move back home with my parents in order to get my business going and at my age living with another female adult in the house (aka my mother!) is driving me to drink. I definitely qualify for federal disaster relief.

The only thing is "I know for sure" the feds will not be coming. Neither is Brad Pitt about to come to "Make it Right." I am on my own. Either I clean up my own mess, and rebuild my own "disaster area," or I wallow in it till the "grim reaper" comes to take me home.

Yes, I've got to fix me. I've got to get kinetic. I've got to become a juggernaut. But where do I begin? How did I get here? Why am I the latest bloomer in the Northeastern United States? Whose life is this anyway? I feel almost like this is somebody else's life, like I'm watching a TV sitcom. This cannot be my life. I did not sign up for this. I signed a different contract and life did not hold up its end of the bargain, at all. Here I am, about a week from my 40th birthday, sitting down to check my e-mail, and having this hot flash that my life is an epic federal state of emergency and I haven't got a clue how it got to be this way. Where to begin to restore order and equilibrium? First of all, why am I not a millionaire? Why aren't I married to a wonderful, successful, kind, loving man who loves me as much as I love him and is not on the "down low"? Why don't I have 1.5 beautiful children sitting in the back seat of my car? Why isn't my career a glowing success? Where's my Jaguar? Why don't I live in one of those homes featured in *So Chic: Glamorous Lives Stylish Spaces?* Huh? What is this?

Ok. Here's what I think needs to happen: First, I need to have a conversation with the woman in the mirror. Then, I need to consult with Oprah, Mr. Trump and Jesus. Then I need to go out there and get my stuff: my money, my husband, my kids, my successful career, my Jaguar, and my home which will be featured in Elle Decor (and not necessarily in that order!) The experiences I've had and the people I've observed and the many self-improvement books I've read better come through for me now. I am ready to take action because I know that nothing will happen unless I do something. Not even Jesus will lift a finger to help me till I take action. So I need to map out strategies right now. I need to create my life. I need to uncreate the mess. I need to start living my "best life." But nothing and nobody better stand in my way. Cause I mean business. Is that clear? So, do you want to come along for the ride?

    Yes? Ok. Here we go.

Note to Reader

This book came out of a personal dialogue I had with myself and a few imaginary "friends" each of whom happens to be a huge icon, celebrity, philanthropist, philosopher and billionaire, about how to "live my best life." I am talking of course about Oprah Winfrey, Donald Trump and Jesus—although I suspect that Jesus has a lot more than just a few measly billion dollars. When I was through talking (in my journal), it occurred to me that this might make an interesting book and that it might inspire a similarly situated person who is feeling a bit behind the curve.

This dialogue is one that is ongoing. In searching my soul to figure out how to achieve this objective, it occurred to me that Oprah coined the phrase (well, she trademarked it) but Donald and Jesus are also leading examples of people who live, or have lived, their best life.

Thus, if I want answers on how to live my best life, I simply have to look to these three masters (and a few others) for guidance and inspiration. Somewhere in the medley of their life philosophies, I am convinced, is the answer to my personal conundrum.

Just so you know, I have never actually met or spoken in person with Ms. Winfrey, Mr. Trump or Mr. Jesus. I just want to make that crystal clear. My conversations with them are totally imaginary and are based on my observations of them in the press, reading about them in books and magazines (and in the case of Jesus—The New Testament) and any other sources that are available to the public. So please, please, please don't tell these people I said I met them or spoke to them.

In the case of Donald Trump in particular, I just want to say that I've read some of his books and I watched a few Apprentice Shows. I've patterned his responses after things he's said and a lot of what I write may be what he actually said or some sort of paraphrase of what he said. A lot of it I just made up. Nothing is this book is based on an actual conversation with him.

As for Oprah, I have watched a lot of Oprah shows over the years. I don't get to see a lot of her now because I am busy working when she is on. But she is a cultural icon and international celebrity. It is hard to escape a sound bite from her almost anytime you walk by a television set. I am totally inspired by her. I have the greatest respect for her work. She is one of my heroes. I based what I wrote on her TV persona and what I think she might say if I had actually spoken with her.   Where Jesus is concerned, it is all based on what I remember being taught in Sunday school as a girl growing up. I know there are many people who take their religious beliefs very seriously. I hope I do not offend anyone by anything I say here. That certainly is not my intention. I am a believer too. I hope what I say is taken in the spirit it was intended and that no one feels the need to accuse me of blasphemy. (Oh, and if hearing the word "God," or talking about "financial abundance" makes you itch or angry, don't read this book because these words appear in it in quite a few places and I don't want to upset your equilibrium.)

Think Big

One
A private jet

I need a plane!

I really mean it. Oh my God. Please somebody help me. I just got off of a 19 hour bus ride from Penn Station in NYC to Atlanta, Georgia. It's the eve of my 40th birthday and I accompanied my mother to her Mac mansion in the South, by bus, because she is afraid of flying since 911 and didn't want to take the bus ride alone; and neither she nor I know how to drive a car. A cabin on Amtrak would have been the only civilized alternative, but in my mother's defense, Amtrak was sold out and there was no other way but by bus.

Let's just get one thing straight: 19 hours on the bus, from NYC to Georgia, is for the birds. It's not that I think I'm above anything or anybody, but by the time you get to be my age, you should travel in style, with your Louis Vuitton luggage and Prada heels, on a private jet, or don't travel. If you think I'm wrong, just ask Valentino. Ask Oprah. Ask Mr. Trump. None of these people would get on the bus unless they were filming a TV show. Valentino probably wouldn't get on it even if he were doing a show. He only travels on private jets and I don't blame him.

I am not disparaging the bus company but the thing with it is, if you are not hyper aggressive, you won't get on the bus, you won't arrive with your luggage and you won't end up in the right destination or with the right cohorts with whom you originally set out. This could prove to be very inconvenient.

It is very dog eat dog; a real jungle on the bus, every man and woman for him or herself. In this case, it's me for myself and all my mother's bags which needed to be safely put at the bottom of the bus, while she hopped on to "hold our seats." This really annoyed me. Because I told her before she did this that I did not want to do the ton of suitcases on the bus thingy. I specifically warned her that if she insisted on bringing more bags than she could handle on her own, namely a carryon and her pocket book, that she would be on her own with them because I would not look at her never mind assist her with any of it. And I didn't care if that made me sound like a monster. I had to stop her before she even thought about it.

Everybody over-packs on the bus. What they can't stuff overhead, they shove underneath the bus. You have never seen such enormous, bulging suitcases in your life. I don't understand it.

What are they packing in those cases? And where is it that they are going to wear all of this stuff?

My mother is the type who thinks nothing of packing ten bags for a four day trip. She's done it before and so she knows what a horror show it is. She enlists everybody she can to assist her with this debacle. We've all been wise enough to boycott the bus for the last three years. But this year, as I said, we did not book our itineraries soon enough so we were left with only the bus in the mad holiday rush.

In any event, she went ballistic and accused me of treating her like a child when I insisted that she only take two small carry-ons. She huffed and puffed and insisted that she was not taking anything more than she needed and that if I didn't want to help her, she would just ask strangers for their assistance. Obviously, she knows I could not in good conscience stand by while my own mother struggles with bags and begs strangers for their help. I'm a dutiful Capricorn, she knows this. This guilt trip is exactly what I don't need at this point in my life; for Chris sakes this time tomorrow I will be a forty year old woman! I'm too old for this.

I wish I was better able to deal with her. She always manages to make me feel guilty. She is completely unreasonable and I can never seem to get old enough that I can stop being her child. She says I treat her like a child. But she treats me like a child and she also acts like a child to get her way. You should have seen her when I told her to only take what she needed. She completely fell out. I could only sit there helplessly and stare at her.

It was a sign of things to come. Tempers are routinely hot on the bus. Travelers have been known to get kicked off buses and left in wrong states due to belligerent behavior that is caused by too cramped, ergonomically incorrect seats, overcrowding, a voyage that is usually interminable, and all that luggage! Only the Devil could enjoy this experience. And it's not as if the people who ride the bus understand the art of the queue. They're usually like a bunch of charging bulls trying to get out of the gate first, cause if they don't they could be left somewhere like Baltimore Travel Plaza, Charlotte, Raleigh, or Richmond with a whole bunch of pissed off people. They are going to pull, shove, push and jump the line and get away with it if you don't get aggressive and demand they get their butts and their valises to the back. Since there is no security check, this latter part is extremely perilous, I must warn you.

In any event, guess what? My mother did only bring two bags (in addition to two pieces of carryons) but they were ginormous. And guess what else? She was completely unable to carry them. So guess who was left to deal with those heavy, overstuffed valises for 19 hours from New York to Atlanta, lugging them on and off various bus changes and having to make sure that nobody accidentally walked off with them?

So chaotic! To think I really wanted to turn 40 peacefully and tranquilly so that I could think about my mid-life crisis. You know what? I need to buy myself a private jet. Oprah and Donald Trump have private jets (unlike some other celebrities who can only afford to rent a private plane from companies like Netjets, these two actually own their planes.) There's a reason that Oprah and Donald have their own planes and I'm sure it has something to do with their mother. I should get my pilot license too, and then I should fly her to Georgia in my plane myself. Trust me she'll be so petrified with me at the helm, she won't be able to speak!

If I talked to Oprah, Donald and Jesus I think they would say the following:

Oprah: I've traveled commercially for years. When I started out doing news in Chicago, I couldn't even dream of having my own private jet. You have to remember I am just a little girl from Kosciusko Mississippi who grew up in the ghettos of Milwaukee. We had linoleum floors when I was growing up. My mother was a maid. I remember the first time I saw Diana Ross and the Supremes on TV I called all my friends yelling, "Colored people on TV! Colored people on TV!" That's where I came from. And here I am I own a fleet of private jets. I employ a fleet of private pilots, and Jet Blue just called wanting to know if I wanted to save the airline. I always dreamed big. But I didn't dream this big. Who knew? But seriously I've flown commercial and I've had a private jet. A private jet is *way* better. This I know for sure. I say live your best life!

Donald Trump: In my line of business, time is money and money is time. I need to be able to get from NY to Vegas, to California, to Dubai and then off to Slovenia to see Melania's parents, and back to Trump Tower to shoot my TV show--in very short notice. I can't afford flight delays. You've got to have a private jet or you're just not competitive when you're in my world. Competition is everything. Competition is business. Competition is life. You can't compete if your flight is delayed, or if god forbid you're on a bus. Is this a joke?

Jesus: I have traveled by foot, I have used a donkey. These days I need a real time solution to my omnipresent travel requirements now that the Father requires that I travel through planets, galaxies, constellations and universes. That's why I asked the Father for wings and he gave me wings. The Lord thy God is mighty and can do mighty and miraculous things. Remember: Ask and it shall be given unto you. Amen.

When I put it all together, my grand conclusion is: If you ask for something, even if it is far fetched and beyond your imagination, you might get it; so be careful what you ask for. Also, never take the bus for 19 hour trips across States. And while you're at it, learn to control your mother! (Shhh. Don't tell my mother I said this.)

Two
The Heavy-hitter mind-set

I didn't use to think big enough and that is why my life is the size it is. That is why I don't have a private jet. That is why I can't even imagine having a private jet. I made a habit of thinking smaller than I should, of limiting myself to what was "realistic." Getting to 40 changes everything. I know that if I continue on the current trajectory, exactly everything will remain the same in my life. I will remain in dire straits. Why continue with the same way when I can see that dire straits are the outcome? This is insane. Look, Oprah always says, "Live your best life." True, that's a tall order. But what is the alternative? Living your worse life? If we are going to be alive anyway, we might as well live grandly, richly and happily. Right? I need to start thinking like a heavy-hitter, like Oprah. Maybe a private jet is not that far fetched after all.

We all have free will. Everything begins in our thoughts. Knowing this, everyone should know they are free to think as big as they choose. They are free to be a heavy-hitter in their minds. We all have the capacity to achieve anything we set our minds to. It is myth that there is anything that a person cannot do, if that person is determined enough and puts their mind to it with enough intensity. If a person can think of something, if they can conceive something, they can achieve that thing. Period. How do you think people built planes? How do you think people learned to perform heart surgeries? How do you think Ben Affleck won an Academy Award for Best

Screen Play? These accomplishments came from big thoughts. They came from believing that the impossible was not only possible, it was also probable. They came from not thinking that something was too "far-fetched" to accomplish. They came from being audacious. One has to have a lot of audacity to get from where one is to where one dreams of going.

It is important to avoid associating with negative people who will try to convince you that you're a nut just because your aspirations, imagination and goals are big. Don't allow small minded people to rain on your parade. They will keep you down on purpose, just so you don't get ahead of them and before you know it, all this time gets wasted and you wake up and you're forty and there's nothing to show for your life. Some people are very cunning. But they act in smart ways by making you feel bad or inferior or wrong about what ever it is you desire or are convicted about. They know you're on to something great or going places so they thwart you on purpose.

Be that as it may, it is important not to be arrogant, boastful or filled with conceit when you do achieve your objectives. It is important to be humble and to keep things in perspective. It is important to remember that "what is invisible is just as powerful--even more powerful--than what is visible." It is a terrible mistake not to acknowledge and respect that which is invisible. It is a terrible mistake to think you are IT. As I age, I am seeing that it is completely arrogant and idiotic and obtuse of me to fail to give The Invisible its due. This failure is what will keep my life small.

If I talked to Oprah, Donald Trump and Jesus I think they would say the following:

Oprah: Live your best life! How many times do I have to say this for it to get through your head? Do I need to get on a bus and go to every town in America and remind everybody? Cause I will if I have to. I will get on my bus and make a tour and come to your town and remind you. In order to live your best life, you have to think big.

More is possible. Go for more! Rich is better than poor. Trust me. I know for sure. Now, free BMWs for everybody in the audience!

Donald Trump: Just read my book, *Think Big and kick Ass*. That's all I have to say to you.

Jesus: With all due respect to Mr. Trump, just read *my* book, *The Holy Bible*. That's all I have to say to you. And remember: The Lord thy God is the Alpha and the Omega. Apply this knowledge to the size of your life. You can do all things through Christ who strengthens you—if you ask for strength. You are created in the image and likeness of God. Be like God. Blessed be God. Blessed be his Holy name. Amen.

When I put it all together, my grand conclusion is: The size of a person's best life is directly correlated to how he or she thinks. Before one can kick ass, one has to think she can kick ass. One has to think big. The Alpha and the Omega is vast. If we all only think as big as a small fraction of that, our thoughts will be enormous. Then the size of our lives will start to correspond to the enormity of our thoughts.

Three
God is rich (and you can be too)

If we are poor—here, here—it is not because we are blessed. I have finally figured that out. It is not because God loves us so much that he has made us poor. Poverty is the gateway to so much that is not good such as crime, stress, disease, exploitation, broken dreams, inferior schools, and trans fats. God did not make anybody poor. If we are poor it is through our choices which come from our thoughts. (Read *The Science of Getting Rich* and you will see what I mean.) If our entire country is poor, it comes from the collective thoughts of the citizens. If our entire continent is poor it comes, once again, from collective thoughts.

We may think we are poor because of others who have exploited us. But could it be we are poor because we did not spend enough time and energy *thinking* about protecting what we have? If our possessions are well protected, we cannot be so easily exploited. In this world, one has to constantly *think* and *rethink* how to protect what one has, and then how to expand what one has to even more. There's a time to party and there is a time to work hard thinking about how to protect your stuff; there's a time to grow your stuff; there's a time to expand your stuff. Everybody is a potential pirate of your stuff!

Change your thoughts, change your circumstances. Because God had nothing to do with your current circumstances if you find yourself poor with nothing. God does not know what poor is. God is the richest man in the entire universe. He's wired exclusively with rich DNA. He only knows rich. God is so rich that if you put all the riches that we can see and quantify in the world together—I mean ALL of it—we still cannot tap .0000000000001% of the net worth of God. God is so rich, there is no human number than can quantify his bank account balance, never mind his passive income and other investments.

What is the currency one would even use to put a value to EVERYTHING? For starters, what is the dollar value of the sun? Who on Earth could buy the sun that warms Earth? Who on Earth has enough resources to afford that? When you are through doing the math, start quantifying the value of those things you cannot see. That's likely to be an even bigger number. Oh, so you thought there is nothing that is invisible? Just because we can't see oxygen doesn't mean it doesn't exist. How much would you pay for a day's supply of oxygen? What is the value of oxygen? Can you even imagine what man would do if he were able to suction all the oxygen in the air into tanks and put a price on it? Look at all the trouble oil wells have caused all because man can see the oil and they will destroy nations just to have control of it. Perhaps that is why God made it so that we can't see oxygen. If man could see and sell oxygen things would be really chaotic on the Earth. Actually, we'd all be dead.

God is very smart. That is why he owns everything. God owns everything that Donald Trump has, he owns everything Oprah has, he owns everything Bill Gates has; he owns *everything*. He owns what we can see and he owns what we can't see. That is why he is rich. He only gives out temporary leases, so we only get to enjoy it but for time so that we don't completely destroy it all with misuse, misappropriation, and abuse; and then we die.

God is the ultimate investment bank. He trades in oxygen, nitrogen, and priceless commodities. This man is very detail oriented. He wanted everything right. He used the right colors, textures, forms, patterns and concepts to make his world and commodities. And forget about the materials he uses. No human has yet created any of these materials which are so rare, expensive and exclusive.

God deposited gold, diamonds, Silver, jade, rubies, coal, copper and aluminum into the crust of his Earth. He dropped oil wells all over the Middle East so that people can have cars and heat their homes. He deposited fresh water lakes, brooks and ponds that provide sweet water to quench our thirst and when the water runs low, he sends snow or rain. He put milk into the breasts of cows so that calves and babies can have something pure and healthy to drink. And isn't it miraculous how bees make honey? How much is all this worth?

He put mink onto the backs of chinchillas and leathery flesh onto the backs of alligators that makes Jimmy Choo and fashionistas salivate. He lavished luscious and exotic fruits onto fruit trees so that we can eat and seduce each other, including grapes which are then used to make the most expensive wines, and apples for our pies. He totally filled up the whole entire place with good gases so that we can breathe and not suffocate from a lack of air; and filled us with carbon dioxide which we breathe out to feed the plants and trees.

Then, he put a sun in the sky to provide us with light, warmth, and good moods.

God is not cheap. God is certainly *not* poor. If he were poor he could not have afforded to make any of the things he has made. We all know that it takes money to buy and make stuff. It takes loads of money to buy God's stuff. God is filthy rich! Oh, he feels for and sympathizes with the poor. He loves the poor just like he loves the abundant. He feels bad that the poor can't see the truth of how they are capable of changing their circumstances. He expects those who have figured out how to be abundant to assist those who can't understand how to do it. But it doesn't change the fact that he is rich. Are you hearing me? I got to be forty years old and it came to me in an epiphany: GOD IS RICH. God reads rich. God thinks rich. God sleeps rich. God smells rich. God creates rich. God only knows rich. And the wonderful thing is he created us in his "image and likeness." He wants us to be like him; he wants us to be abundant in every way just like he is. How can we accomplish this? Who knows? I just think we need to figure out a way to take nothing and CREATE something. The key is in *creating* stuff. That's all God does. He creates. How do we create? What do we create? I think we need to start by figuring what we are good at, and go from there.

If I talked to Oprah, Donald Trump and Jesus I think they would say the following:

Oprah: I've always said on this show, you've got to live your best life. I believe in God. I believe he is rich. I believe all abundance comes from him. If you are not abundant you have to search within to find the reason why not. Get yourself together, girl! Get off your late blooming behind and go for yours. Don't put if off another day. Being poor is not a bad thing. But it's not your best life. Start living your best life now! Figure out what you're good at, and do it. Find your abundance.

Donald Trump: I don't discuss my religious beliefs, those are private. But I do believe that you create your own wealth and you create your own poverty.

Jesus: The Lord your God is mighty, wealthy and full of abundance. Follow his way and you too shall be abundant. But blessed is he who considereth the poor. Amen.

When I put it all together my grand conclusion is: Abundance is a limitless resource. Our "best life" is a life of abundance; our "best life" is for us to create; we create our abundance with the grace of

God; God is abundant and wants every person to be abundant; but he expects those who are abundant to help those who are not.

Four
Expand to infinity

Recently I heard somewhere that scientists were finding new planets and galaxies that they didn't know existed before. This to me was very fascinating. Are scientific equipment getting better so as to enable scientists to see things they couldn't see before, but which have always existed? Or is it that these things were not there before, but were in fact CREATED while we were busy looking in the other direction thinking what we could discern with our eyes and telescopes and probes is all there is and ever will be? I wondered whether scientists allow for the possibility that the Universe self-reproduces, that it expands and stretches its own dimensions and scope, in a totally unscientific way, or whether scientist believe that it all comes down to science only?

You get to live as long as I have and you realize, unequivocally, that not only *must* there be a God, not only is he rich, but this dude is BIG. God is a *big* god! God is so big he transcends measurement. I am starting to think that his bigness is not static. I think he continues to self-reproduce; he continues to expand. He is a rich, big, *expanding* tour de force! I know I'm starting to sound like a religious fanatic with all my talks of God. And it is the funniest part of this because I am not religious at all. I have really just stumbled upon this truth and I feel compelled to say it out loud, to share with anyone who wants to hear. I know that this is not what everybody believes. I am not in the business of trying to convert anyone. If you are convinced, great. If you are not convinced, fine.

I am really fascinated by the notion that God is still creating as we speak and his Kingdom in infinite and that his infinity keeps expanding, keeps getting bigger and bigger and will always keep getting bigger and that human brain can never and will never fully grasp the mystery and miracle of it and will *never* catch up to it. I think that God is amused by science. I think scientists make his eyes twinkle mischievously. God is not science. God is not math. God is not History. He is not philosophy. He is not religion. God just IS. (And please don't you dare go ask former President Bill Clinton to define "is" because he has no clue what the meaning of IS, is; nobody does!)

This elasticity and expandability of God, in my view, is instructive because it tells me that success and achievement require flexibility, pliability and stretch-ability. One cannot afford to be rigid. One can never dare think one is done. There is always something else to do, there is always somewhere else to go, and there is always something else to try. There is no one path to success. There is no one path to achieving a goal. There are many different ways to skin a cat. There are infinite possibilities. Thus, one must keep trying to expand, keep redefining limits and boundaries, keep getting bigger, keep stretching oneself as much as one can, even if sometimes you think you've reached capacity and are about to burst. You are not going to burst. There is no capacity except death. And who really knows what happens then? Maybe the party is just beginning.

So what is the lesson? One has to stretch oneself, go outside one's "comfort zone" literally take on different forms. As we learn one thing, perfect another. We can then use it all as leverage to go to the next level, create the next thing. It's a revelation, realizing this; so fascinating! Now, all I personally have to do is apply this revelation to my late-bloomer-federal-state-of-emergency-aka-my-life. And I'm going to be rich both spiritually and financially and have all the desires of my heart!

If I talked to Oprah, Donald Trump and Jesus I think they would say the following:

Oprah: Girl, fill yourself up! Expand yourself. Live your best life. Look at me. I am about to expand myself from what I have now, to owning my own TV Network called OWN. Fifteen years ago I wrote that in my journal. Now it is manifesting. It takes time to expand. But you must expand. You cannot stop growing. You can never stop growing and expanding. There is no way that you can live your best life if you are not expanding.

Donald Trump: Like I said, I am never satisfied. I always want more. I want to do more. I work. I never stop working. I never stop creating. I can't stop. Sometime I feel condemned to keep going. It is like a condemnation. Sometimes my creativity and drive is like a *condemnation*. I do not understand laziness. I do not understand accepting less than my best or anybody else's best. Look at my buildings. Each is a bigger masterpiece than the one that came before. I want to have the tallest building in the world one day. There was a time that 40 Wall was the tallest building in the World. Now it is the tallest building in downtown Manhattan. Did you know I got that building for free? I own the tallest residential building in NYC, if not the world. I want a building that touches the clouds. I want a building that really transcends time and space. That is what I aim for. I am going to build the biggest, tallest most spectacular building in the world and it's going to be in United Emirates. I have Ivanka over there scoping out the land as we speak. We are expanding. But I want to expand not just globally but cosmically. I want to build something on the moon. That is what I want. That is what will make me feel satisfied. I think.

Jesus: My father made the Heavens. My father made the mustard seed. Faith as big as a mustard seed can move mountains. Imagine what would happen if you expanded your faith to be as big as the Heavens? Amen.

When I put it all together, my grand conclusion is: A person's best life is a life that expands and does not remain static; a person's best life is one that keeps getting better. Never skimp on creativity; always have faith that you can create the life you want. Always keep busy; never stop trying to reach your peak. Never be satisfied with less than your best.

Five
Carrie's Manolo Blaniks were not a type of 401K

Carrie Bradshaw was a thirty-something clotheshorse and shoes horse whom I greatly admired for any number of reasons. Namely, each of her stuff was an investment piece. Her most prized asset, Mr. Big, was the hottest man within a thousand mile radius. Not only was he hot, he was also rich and could loan her a deposit to buy her apartment when it turns out that she had no savings on account of all the Manolo Blaniks she purchased over the years.

Carrie was hot, young, sexy, blonde, thin, talented and sexually confident; the perfect match for Mr. Big. She could afford Manhattan rents, and had famous friends who could invite her to amazing soirees, including designers, writers and politicians. Darling, I am no Carrie Bradshaw.

But I was a profligate spender in my youth and I paid the price for buying all those outfits when I should have been buying stock in Microsoft and Apple and contributing to my employer matched 401K. Back then I could barely tell the difference between cashmere and polyester. So it's not as if I have all the stuff I bought to look at and wear now. They've mostly been donated to thrift.

I wish somebody had sat me down and explained to me the importance of putting money aside for later years, of growing my nest egg, and increasing my net worth instead of spending all my money on clothes. I would probably be a millionaire by now. It was only after I filed bankruptcy, in my early thirties, that I finally understood the price of being a spendthrift. It was only after that "financial shipwreck" that I sought to try to put a few dollars away before I started to spend.

Don't get me wrong, I am still a spender. I am wired to spend, spend, and spend. I'm like Paris Hilton who's wired to party, party, and party. But Paris is an heiress and a shrewd business woman who gets paid over half a million dollars a pop just to attend a party. She laughs all the way to the bank. I do not get paid to spend like a damn fool and when I go to the bank my face is usually wearing a grimace.

This foolish tendency to spend every dime may have been cute when I was young. But it is not cute when you are a middle aged woman with nothing. The trouble is, most young people don't understand that you're only as financially secure in middle age as the way you spent your youth. In the end, everybody has their wake up call.

Every financially independent person, I have learned, is literate with respect to balance sheets, income statements, the tax consequences of certain transactions, savings accounts, retirement savings, interest rates, prime rates, IRA's, money market accounts and even more complex concepts like estate planning and generational trusts and educational trusts.

I am not going to kid you. I still don't fully understand the difference between a Roth and a traditional IRA never mind some of this other stuff. But I am getting better with this money thing. I am a lot better than I used to be. I am finally *aware* that I will continue to be a financial slave unless I make serious changes in how I handle my money. And one of the changes I have to make is in how I think about money, how much money I save and invest, and much money remains untouched even when the proverbial #$@% hits the fan.

If I talked to Oprah, Donald Trump and Jesus I think they would say the following:

Oprah: I've done a ton of Oprah Shows on this issue. I've had everybody on here talking about this, Suze Orman, David Bach, everybody. We all learned about the Latte Factor here on the Oprah Show. How many times do I have to say this? You have to save your money. You have to respect your money. It's very hard to do much without money. It's about living your best life. Sure, the best things in life are free, but for everything else you need money.

Donald Trump: "Educate yourself on making proper investments with your money." Don't leave you money to any of those genius experts, all those guys who don't have enough money to pay their rent. Ask the expert to show you his balance sheets then talk about what he can do for you and your money. Handle your money like a pro. If you're a man, buy Brioni suits. Or buy my shirts from my line at Macy's. It's a good deal for the quality, the best of its kind. If you like steak, buy my beef. But other than that, don't waste money on clothes. Oh, and invest in a good pair of shoes. I've learned it makes a big difference with how much money you make if you look like quality when you go on the interview. Buy everything I tell you and you will be fine.

Jesus: A fool hoards riches on Earth. Behold thy real riches are in heaven. Amen.

When I put it all together my grand conclusion is: Where money is concerned, it is important to keep things in perspective; there is more to life than just money. That doesn't mean money is not critically important. So long as we have life, money will be critically important. Everyone should be educated about money, like any other subject, in school. That way, people can start to make good, sound, financial decisions and not plummet into a financial landmine through ignorant decision-making and rash behavior. Yet, it is foolish to think that money is all that there is. In the end, we will not be judged by how much money was in our bank accounts.

Six
Watch your pennies (and put notes in a jar)

In one of Donald Trump's books, it might be *Think like a Billionaire* but I think it could have been "*How to Get Rich*, he talks about watching pennies. He talks about the fact that even though he's a billionaire he still watches his pennies he still pays attention to what things cost. Oprah Winfrey, another billionaire, talks about respecting money enough to watch how you put it into your wallet. She says, "Do not crumple up the money and have a messy wallet. Respect money." I remember watching that show and getting goose bumps when she said that because my own wallet is often in a state of abject chaos. Mostly it is filled with crumpled up receipts and bank slips, and the few odd notes. I have suffered from an ailment I call "Empty Wallet Syndrome" in the past. It meant I have not been happy till every dollar in my wallet is spent.

Lately I have not only been watching my pennies, I have also been watching my notes. I started to empty my wallet of notes every night and putting them in a jar to see how much money I have at the end of each week--money which would have been spent and squandered before I decided to be more conscious of my habits. It is incredible how much money I "save" now that I am putting my notes in a jar. It helped me to be disciplined and to take out only as much as I need everyday. Not to make excuses, but I am one of those people who grew up in a culture that taught me that having money is bad. I grew up in the Catholic Church. Nuns and priests actually take vows of poverty. In Sunday school you are told stories of a Deity who wants to keep us poor out of love. "Blessed are the poor," they would say. As a result, I grew up around people who believed that poverty was a badge of honor. I grew up in the Caribbean and we all believed that only poor people will go to Heaven and that God only loves poor people, and that it is "harder for a rich man to go to heaven than for a camel to go through the eye of a needle." This teaching is deeply indoctrinated and imbedded into the genetic code of most poor people like myself.

However I have started to think that there is something wrongheaded about thinking God wants us to be poor, and blesses us for it. Jesus did say "blessed are ye who are poor." But what did he mean? I think he meant, "blessed are you *even though* you are poor and you don't have money; I still love you," rather than "blessed are you *because* you are poor and have no money; that is why I love you." There's a difference. It is completely wrongheaded to believe that Jesus meant "blessed are you *because* you are poor." Poverty is not a blessing! Abundance is a blessing! Just as it is important to be spiritually abundant, it is also important to be financially abundant. You can't pay the rent with spirituality. You can't pay the rent with poverty. It is ridiculous to walk around thinking that financial abundance is bad and that all rich people are bad and will rot in hell while all the poor people are in Heaven. There are many good rich people. There are many bad poor people.

It is ironic that while the nuns and priests were taking poverty vows, and teaching us how to love being poor, the Bishops and Popes and Cardinals were eating like kings and living rich. And I say that with all due respect. I am not just hitting Catholics either. In almost any organized religion, the pastors, elders, rabbis and bishops live much more abundantly than the congregation. They do it largely through tithing, the ultimate form of passive income, the kind of income you need a lot of in order to get rich. Let me tell you something: Religion is a huge money making enterprise. It is big business. And it feeds on the poor and unenlightened.

Don't get me wrong: I love the fact that I still live in a world where all the churches have not been turned into condominiums. If all the churches disappeared, it would be an awful thing. I like that there are churches even though I go only once or twice per year. There is something comforting about seeing churches, synagogues, mosques and other places of worship all around. The answer is not to get rid of churches. However, people have to wake up and see what is going on in many churches and how what goes on (and what is being said) in their church keeps them in the poor house--and then they have to start holding themselves accountable for their own participation, if what is being said and practiced, does not comport with the true intentions of God.

It is the intention of God that each person reaches his or her full potential, that each person enjoys abundance, including financial abundance. It is also the intention of God that there is no waste of the abundance he bestows upon us. As rich as he is, God is not wasteful. With all his abundance, there is no excess to his creation. Look around you. There is no gaudiness in nature. There is no gluttony. There is nothing left unfinished. There is only perfection. Perfect beauty. That is why I think I need to watch my pennies because God is the kind of guy who would do that. He would watch his pennies and he will bless me for watching mine, and for putting notes in a jar at the end of each day and not spending every dime like a mindless fool.

If I talked to Oprah, Donald Trump and Jesus I think they would say the following:

Oprah: Clean out your wallet, Girl! You can't live your best life is your wallet is a mess!

Donald Trump: I am actually a very simple guy who lives a very simple life. True, I have a private jet. True, I also have a helicopter for jaunts to Atlantic City. True, I live in Trump Tower--the best building on Fifth Avenue in NYC. True, I am on the Forbes List of billionaires. True, I have a driver and I get driven around in limos (except for that night in the rain when I went to meet those bankers in the 90s when I was in deep deep financial doo doo.) True, I have servants and nannies and personal secretaries and doormen. True, I shop at Asprey and Harry Winston when I want little baubles for my exquisite babe/wife--the Exquisite Melania. But, really, I am a very simple guy. I am a down to earth kind of approachable kind of a guy. My favorite dinner is potato chips and I shop at the local Korean deli. I get bargain socks on wholesale and I shop at Duane Reade for toiletries. I am not going to waste my money on packaging just because it's served up by Madison Avenue and Bergdorf Goodman. The only time I splurge is when I buy gifts for Melania. She's very soothing so she gets great heirlooms.

Jesus: A fool and her money are soon parted. Waste not, want not, saith the Lord. Amen.

When I put it all together, my grand conclusion is: Respect money; value money enough not to waste it on nonsense, lest it runs out and leave you broke.

Put away childish things

Seven
Mistakes are teachable moments

The only person who has never made a mistake is Jesus, and that is debatable because obviously, the fact that he got crucified suggests that he must have made a big mistake somewhere and stepped on some wrong toes belonging to somebody somewhere who had a lot of power and who didn't exactly have a particularly great sense of humor.

We all make mistakes. Mistakes are simply teachable moments. It is how we learn. Donald Trump made many mistakes, especially in the early nineties when he was jet setting in Europe with super models and not paying attention to his Organization's bottom line. He nearly went bankrupt and I suspect that might have had something to do with the fact that he had to get rid of his world famous yacht. Plus, he lost Marla—the Georgia Peach. That must have been tough.

Oprah made mistakes too. I have heard her say on her show, "I have many regrets and one of them is an affair I had with a married man." It was shocking to know that even Oprah could have fallen victim to a smooth operator and lothario. Everybody errs, it is human. The important thing, I think, is to learn from the mistakes and not to repeat them because the first time is a mistake. The second time, with the same mistake, is character.

I have made my own mistakes. As a result, there a few things I "know for sure." Actually, there are sixteen:

First, never believe a married man when he tells you he needs you and is not, and never was, attracted to his wife. And that he was always more attracted to his wife's mother than to his own wife. The only thing to do when such a loser appears is run. Because he's not only a cheat, he's also a liar and he's also a used car sales man who's selling a lemon. And on top of it all, nobody blames the salesman for his treachery. They blame the woman for buying the car. Surely there are better things to do with your assets than buy this defective merchandise?

Second, when you have money, even if it is a little bit of money, find a way to save a little something out of the little bit, no matter what. And don't spend it come what may even when many justifiable reasons present themselves, as they are guaranteed to do. Do not be rash with money. "Money is a source of energy" which must be respected or it will diss you and go away and leave you poor and bankrupt and your Fico Score will be low for a very long time.

Third, people will only respect you if you refuse to be disrespected. So stand up. Put your foot down and speak your mind. It doesn't have to be at the top of your lungs though. You can do it calmly. Then when you walk out of the room (with your butt all tight and your shoulders back) after putting them in their place for disparaging your work and you leave them standing there with their mouths open because you were so classy, it's infinitely more enjoyable in the aftermath than if you had screamed, "get the #@$% out of my office and don't ever set foot back in here you despicable head lice!" at the top of your lungs.

Fourth, your life is up to you. It is yours to create. And even more profoundly, you can keep wiping the slate clean and start over like a sculptor. You are not stuck in any one way or mold, especially if that way does not work for you. You can change. Change is not always easy, and it takes time, but it can be done if it is what the heart desires. Change is ALWAYS possible, so long as one remains creative and open, and so long as one is not dead.

Fifth, everything counts. There is a cause and effect to everything under the sun. Every act has a consequence. Everything has a price. And if there is a Heaven, all the better, but God exacts payment right here on Earth (and he can be a relentless bill collector!)

Sixth, you are responsible for yourself. Nobody is to blame if your life is a complete mess. But everybody is to be praised if you make a success of it. That's the way the ball hops. So, it is wise to choose everything carefully, including friends, lovers, habits and addictions. Better not to have any addictions, even if it's just overindulgence in profanity.

Seventh, it is true that we all have free will.

Eight, it is not enough to mind your business, keep your mouth shut and stay under the radar. It doesn't mean you will stay out of trouble. Trouble can come knocking on your door even though you are inside watching TV and didn't do anything to solicit it. So it is crucial to watch your back. Because as Donald Trump would say: "there are bad people in the world who will mess with you just for sport." If you are not paying attention to the back end, but busy looking only in one direction like a good, responsible, naive little girl (or boy), they could kick you in the ass and knock you on your face into the mud and next thing you know you'll be chewing on dirt or biting on a bullet.

Ninth, sometimes you have to play dead just to live to fight another day.

Tenth, it is important to stay focused and control your mind. You really are your thoughts.

Eleventh, it is important to practice humility and not to be wrong and strong or right with might.

Twelfth, it is important to live with intensity because this really is it. It is not an audition for Broadway or American Idol. One must find a way to live intensely and fully and happily and peacefully.

Thirteenth, happiness and depression are both choices. You get to choose. Which will it be?

Fourteenth, to err once is a human mistake, but to make the same mistake twice is a character flaw.

Fifteenth, no amount of cosmetics can fix a rotten heart.

Sixteenth, true peace is possible, so long as you get in the habit of living in a way that does not violate your conscience.

If I talked to Oprah, Donald Trump and Jesus I think they would say the following:

Oprah: Regrets are the result of bad judgment in your youth. But it is important to recognize the teachable moments in our lives. A lot of who we are is shaped in childhood. That is why I always say, parenting is the hardest job. It is such a big responsibility. That is why I wanted to have the school in South Africa. I am the surrogate mother for my girls, all 150 of them. I take this responsibility very seriously. I wish I could protect them from all regrets. When I retire,

I am going to move to South Africa and live near my school. The Oprah Winfrey Academy for Girls I am going to eat from the same utensils as my girls. I want to experience what they experience. But in the end, I believe you should live your best life no matter what mistakes you made when you were young and dumb. Do not let your past define you. Live your best life!

Donald Trump: Don't waste time on regrets. Just think big, watch your back, have fun, don't be a schmuck, don't drink, don't smoke, don't do drugs, don't allow any addictions, be disciplined, get a beautiful woman (or man) who will pose on top of your piano, watch your bottom line, and work hard. Life at the top is great!

Jesus: Follow my example and live in peace forever with no regrets; you will inherit everything on the Earth. That is the will of my Father. Amen.

When I put it all together, my grand conclusion is: Mistakes come from bad judgment; but mistakes teach us important life lessons. These lessons save us from bigger screw ups later down the road. It doesn't make sense to dwell on mistakes, however, only to learn from them and apply them in the future; at the same time, some mistakes are avoidable. If we do the right thing from the very start we'll have a whole lot less regrets to talk about in the future.

Eight
Put away childish things

"When you're a child, you act like a child and on becoming a man, you put away childish things." This quote is from the Bible, although I don't know the passage and I don't know if it was Jesus or some prophet from the Old Testament who said it. But a few months ago, Oprah said this on her show. I have heard this verse all my life and only now does it make sense: Being forever youthful is good. But being forever childish is not.

Some of us end up having this extended adolescence because we are afraid to grow up. We keep deferring it, till we wake one day and realize we are so far behind the rest of the pack, it is not altogether clear we can ever catch up. We end up not being as productive and responsible as we could have been or should have been. I know I am guilty of this. Maybe this subconscious fear of growing up is the reason I have never really had a meaningful relationship with a man. I have always not really known how to act around men. My sister accused me just recently of acting like a 16 year old around men. She's right of course. My sexual development was somehow arrested at around age 16. I completely act like a moron in the presence of a man I desire. I am getting better at not trembling, visibly, but I am definitely a juvenile bundle of nerves around men. I don't know what to say around them, I don't know how to act around them. It's totally embarrassing. And I think it factors into the fact that I'm still single.

As 40 approaches, obviously, this has to be put away. There are other things which need to be put away too. By this age, a woman has to be the woman she has become and put away a lot of other things that hold her back and keep her from realizing her full potential. A childish forty year old is not cute. So many women of this age are already grandmothers. It's unimaginable but it's true. Many are on to their second and third marriages. They've had kids, know how to drive and own an SUV. They are worried about paying for their kids' college expenses and paying their mortgage on their three bedroom house in suburbia. They know what it feels like to get a divorce.

When you're a woman, you act like a woman and put away childish things. There are so many ways in which we are childish. (I would speak for myself but misery wants company here.) It could be as simple as being impulsive. Children are impulsive and it's forgivable. But an impulsive forty year old or even a reckless forty year old, is a danger to themselves and society. Recklessness in spending, speaking, decision-making, living, can truly destroy a person's life, or at least set you back a few decades.

Some people are childish in the way they always need the consent and endorsement of others in order to make up their mind about important decisions. A woman is able to make up her own mind. It is not that she does not seek the opinion of others at any time at all, but she makes up her own mind on all important matters and usually, she keeps her big mouth shut about it anyway, and does her own thing. Real women are very secretive, I've noticed. They are often quite mysterious. They are not an open book whom everybody can see coming a mile away. It is important to be more subtle, and not to be the proverbial bull in the china closet. It is also important to have good timing, too.

Being childish could mean having an out of control temper. One has to mellow with age, cut down on the temper tantrums. Two year olds can be excused for tantrums. But at forty, the days for epic meltdowns are long gone. Take it from me: it does not pay to be the emotional woman in the room who loses all control when she doesn't get her way. This is a tough lesson. Sometimes, I think people push my buttons because they know I am prone to melting (especially people who know me, who are close to me.)

I am aware of this, and towards the end of my thirties, I have become better at keeping these tantrums at bay, and expressing my displeasure more constructively. But I am definitely not healed. I definitely need to apply more work and effort to putting this childish thing away. A real woman feels every emotion. But she doesn't completely lose it, even when the situation calls for her to completely lose it. Or if she loses it, she does it as if she is Joan Collins. She speaks in a calm voice as she cuts offenders down to size. She is articulate and exacting. She speaks her mind, stands up for herself. But she does not melt down. She does not lose it. She understands that out of control anger is a weakness. A real woman is strong. A real woman is in control of herself.

We can show our childishness by showing a lack of confidence. It is more than just sexual confidence I am speaking about. It is professional confidence too, and social confidence. But I think the sexual energy is one of the strongest energies human beings possess. And I think if one can get that in order, everything else will fall into place. If we are not sure of ourselves at forty, if we still need to hear from others that we are worthy, sexy, beautiful, in order to feel these things, there's a problem. There's work to do because one should know who one is without needing to hear it from anybody else by forty. One should not need to be reminded constantly by others. A woman should not still need to be convinced like a twenty-five year old that she is enough just the way she is, when she is a grown woman of forty.

If I talked to Oprah, Donald Trump and Jesus I think they would say the following:

Oprah: Know who you are. Live your best life. And grow up, girl. Act your age. You have to be confident, girl. Do not act like a child when you're forty. What's the matter with you? It's not cute, girl. PUT AWAY CHILDISH THINGS. You know, it's so funny but my Best friend Gayle always tells me to grow up. She says, just grow up! What I can honestly say for sure is that I've put away childish things. It all happened at fifty. Once and for all. Something magical happened at my fiftieth birthday party....When I turn sixty, I'm going make it look like thirty! I'll invite everybody from Sidney Poitier, John Travolta, Diana Ross, Quincy Jones, Diane Sawyer, Nelson Mandela, Dr. Phil, Denzel Washington, Barrack Obama, Hillary Clinton, My best friend Gayle, Andre my hairdresser, Tina Turner, Jennifer Anniston, Maya Angelou, Maria Shriver, Tom Cruise...you think Tom Cruise will come? It's going to be great. I am going to make sixty look great. Life is a big, wonderful celebration so long as you put away childish things when its time. We should have a "grow up" slumber party at the Oprah Winfrey Show. That might be fun.

Donald Trump: Timing is everything. "If you don't have good timing, you are going to have major problems in business and in life. " It is okay to ask others for their opinion but do what you think is best. Try to always do the opposite of everything anybody ever tells you. "Be counterintuitive." When it comes to beauty, not everybody is a great beauty. Everybody *can't* be a great beauty. It's a statistical impossibility. Just accept that. "Angelina Jolie is not a great beauty. She's attractive but not a great beauty." George Clooney is short. I have married the most beautiful women in the world. Beauty is something I know. My wife, Melania, is exquisite. That is why I love her. I own the Miss Universe Pageant and it's made me a lot of money because I know beauty. That's why I have the modeling agency, again, because I know beauty. You might think that I got the modeling agency and then I learned about beauty. You are wrong. I knew beauty, and then I got the modeling agency. My daughter Ivanka was a model. She's a great beauty. And she is smart. She went to Wharton. My advice is to do what you know.

Find that thing you are good at and do it well. You have to study your craft. If beauty is your craft, study it well. Read my book, *Think like a Billionaire* and you will understand about beauty. Check out Melania on top of the piano if you need a visual. As for the rest of it, you have to be confident. Know what you're good at and do that. Study your craft. Being the best takes hard work. Don't be childish. Don't be a schmuck. And just remember: Kids can't run billion dollar businesses--unless they're my kids--so grow the heck up!

Jesus: When you're a child, you can speak like a child; you can act like a child. But when you are a grown up, be a grown up lest the Father loses his patience with your nonsense. Amen.

When I put it all together, my grand conclusion is: There comes a time in every person's life when they have to grow up and put away their childish nonsense. I, personally, can't run a billion dollar business if I'm acting like a kid—unless I am a Trump—which I'm not. Therefore, for that and other reasons, it is imperative that I mature emotionally and not just chronologically. That's probably true for most people.

Nine
Write it down!

All the great modern philosophers of life improvement, wealth creation and success, seem to advocate putting down one's goals and desires into writing. They are believers in making lists. I totally agree with them. I have found that when I make lists, even a daily list of things I want to get done, I accomplish more than if I do not make a list. I don't know why that is, but somehow, I am more focused and result-oriented when I make a list than when I just leave myself to the wind. It gives me great pleasure to be able to cross things off my list as *fait accomplis.* Had I made lists of bigger things and life goals I wanted to accomplish, maybe I wouldn't be such an underachiever today. But that's going to change. I am going to see to it that that changes.

Right now, today, I have to make a list of all the things I think keeps me from living the successful life I desire. I am not living my best life, bottom line. It's occurred to me that in order to make real change in my life, it is necessary to start within. Everything starts in the mind. Success and failure, love and hate, ignorance and knowledge, poverty and wealth, health and sickness all of these things, I believe, are mental. They begin in the mind.

While it is tempting to describe myself as a failure just because my life is not perfect and I'm behind the curve, I won't. That is not going to help the situation. Besides, there is a saying that says, "Call no one lucky till he is dead." So I am going to defer putting a summary on my life. It's not over yet. I will admit that I am a late bloomer, but I am not going to say I'm a failure, or a loser, and if you are anything like me, you shouldn't either. Better to say, "I am in the process of manifesting success." Sure, there is a lot of room for improvement in many areas of my life. Sure, self progress probably needs to be sped up a little bit. But if you think about it, there is a lot of abundance and we are all so lucky and blessed for so many reasons and in so many ways. And yes, there is a lot of room of even more blessings and more abundance.

So here I am at forty years of age and I have so many things I need to accomplish, so many things I want, so many goals left unfulfilled. What do you think I'm about to do? I am going to make a list of course. And I'm going to make sure it is specific enough and not too vague so that I don't confuse myself or the Universe. I am going to check it over not once, not twice, but three times just to make sure I don't miss anything because I don't have a lot of time to waste blowing in the wind anymore. I mean business. By the end of this year, I intend to say that this was my most productive year ever…Why don't you also make a list?

If I talked to Oprah, Donald Trump and Jesus I think they would say the following:

Oprah: I am a believer in the written word. I always write things down. I've always kept a journal. In order to live your best life you should do whatever you need to do. My best friend Gayle and I have started to make lists every day. It helps. Especially with all the things I have to do, all the homes I have to keep on top of, the Magazine, the Show, The after-show, The School, the Broadway Plays, Obama, and other production activities. Soon I will have my own network. It will be called OWN. That was on my list for fifteen years. I have to make a list just to wake up in the morning. I have to even list when I get to spend time with Steadman. Thank God for Steadman. Thank God for lists. I am so grateful for lists. I should write that in my gratitude journal.

Donald Trump: Lists are for wimps. I am up at 5:00 in the morning reading the New York Times, the Wall Street Journal, Fortune, Money, all the major players. I'm taking phone calls from everybody from Arnold Schwarzenegger to Joss Stone. I'm doing my sit ups. I'm take notes for my various writing projects but mostly I dictate to my secretary. Norma keeps me organized. She makes the lists and tells me what's on them. There's just too much to do and too little time for me to get into listing.

Jesus: The Father who is in Heaven abhors chaos. It takes a tremendous amount of focus to keep creation in order. Can you imagine the chaos if the father were to stop being so focused and results-oriented? Then you'll have snow in Baghdad, hurricanes in Paris, 100 degree heat in Antarctica. (The latter would be really problematic for Earth so I will see to it that the Father never falls asleep at that wheel!) The Father is the ultimate philanthropist who is in constant demand. There are constant requests for relief aka prayers coming in from a trillion sources by the minute. Everyone from Fidel Castro to Britney Spears to Elvis (Yes, that one) calls in for help. Just yesterday, Hillary Clinton called saying that some guy named Obama cheated her out of the Iowa caucus. As I said, the Almighty Father is very busy. The Father is also a great aesthetician who likes to spend his time building, crafting, shaping, molding and drawing. He's a multitasking project manager with a big generous heart. It is vital that he prioritizes. For that reason, it is and will always be vitally important to write things down. The Lord thy God does not like confusion. The Lord thy God makes lists. The Lord thy God recommends it highly. Blessed be his Holy name. Amen.

When I put it all together, my grand conclusion is: No matter how smart we may think we are, we need to write things down to keep on top of it all; our best life is organized, planned (to some extent) and free from chaos.

Ten
Embrace the Itch

How did you spend your 39th year? Or, if you are not yet 39, I guess I should ask, how will you spend your 39th year?

I spent a whole year preparing myself for my fortieth birthday. For a whole year, instead of embracing being thirty-nine, I told everybody I was forty. I referred to myself as a forty year old, so that I would lessen the impact of forty when it actually happened. It was my way of "embracing" the moment. Great strategy, right? The only thing is that I was never really 39. I never lived 39. Thirty-nine came and went and was never embraced. I lost a whole year. And I can never get it back.

Going forward I want to embrace each day, moment, occasion, opportunity, birthday, emotion and itch. It's like yesterday. I should have embraced the chance to buy that sweet potato pecan pie at Publix I was itching for. If I had bought it, then I could have had a really nice breakfast this morning with my herbal tea and a slice of Pecan Pie for my birthday. Today is actually my birthday. Today is the day I turned 40. All I am having for breakfast is a cup of unsweetened herbal tea. I am sure I will thank myself next week when I get back to New York and I haven't gained ten pounds from all the holiday overeating. But right now, I sure wish I had embraced the urge to buy that delicious looking sweet potato pie at Publix when I had the chance.

It doesn't make sense to have too many "I WISH I HAD" moments going forward into one's fourth decade. By this age, we should living life fully, doing the things we want to do, achieving the things we've always dreamed of, living in the moment with intensity and gratitude. Everybody concurs that this is the age when we reach our prime. I want the prime of my life to be the best time I have ever had in my life. So, what are some of the things I want to do this year and beyond? Well, I badly want a Jaguar, and a few other luxury items like a house in the Hamptons.

Yes, I can hear you saying I am materialistic (and an amusing dreamer.) But I am not going to apologize. That's another thing I want to stop doing in my life, apologizing to people for who I am and what I want and for what I think. No more apologies. I only want to embrace myself. Oprah does not apologize for her private hairdresser and her private chauffeur and her chef and her closet full of Jimmy Choos (given to her by the wives of TV stars) and all her houses. Martha Stewart does not apologize for her farms, and her Upstate New York mansions, and her various TV shows. Sarah Jessica Parker does not apologize for her unbelievable wardrobe full of designer couture and Manolo Blaniks. Donald Trump does not apologize for his three billion dollars and all those buildings with his name on them all over the world. No. They embrace what they have and give thanks for it, and ask for more. And they get more. They have so much, they are constantly giving stuff away, and sometimes they really go all out and start building schools and homes for unfortunate children. That, to me, is what it's all about. I want to be like them. I embrace my desire to be more like them in terms of the abundance they enjoy in their lives. No apologies.

If I talked to Oprah, Donald Trump and Jesus I think they would say the following:

Oprah: Girl, I remember 39 as if it were yesterday. Thirty nine was great fun. I was just coming into my own. I had no idea, though, of the transformation I was about to undergo into my forties and now my fifties. I am here to tell you it does get better with age. Forty was fabulous. Really. But don't rush it. Enjoy every single day. Enjoy every age. Enjoy 39. Live your best life.

Donald Trump: I don't remember what I was doing at forty but I know I was married to Ivana, my first wife, and we may have already bought the Plaza Hotel next to New York's Central Park, the most prime area of Manhattan. I do remember that I was hot stuff. I was up and coming as a major player in New York Real Estate. I always dreamed of being a major player in Manhattan real estate. My father was more of a Queens and Brooklyn guy. I wanted to take Manhattan. But I didn't have any money. I had to make it myself. I had to create a billion dollar business out of nothing. People think I inherited my money. They are wrong. I am a creative genius. I created my wealth out of nothing, with nothing but my bare hands, my good looks and my charm. My taste in women didn't hurt. I was getting a lot of press in my forties. Up and coming tycoon. Emerging real estate titan. Those were the monikers by which I was known and that was only fitting and proper. I single-handedly transformed Midtown into what it is today by being the best at what I did. Exactly what I was doing at 39 or 40, is irrelevant for your purposes. Just know I was creating havoc. And I can tell you that it is important to live hard, with intensity because there's no second chances. Make your own havoc. And play golf. Have a blast.

Jesus: By 30, I had already returned to the father in Heaven so I spent my 40th Birthday in celestial splendor. It was an unbelievable affair, lots of famous people came--people you wouldn't know since they were before your time--but very famous. More famous than Britney Spears, Lindsay and Paris rolled up in one. Live each day as if it was your last. No one knoweth the day or the hour when my father will come again. Amen.

When I put it all together, my grand conclusion is: Nothing is guaranteed. Here today, gone tomorrow. A person's best life means that they make a point of enjoying each day, each moment. It means they squeeze as much living as they can into every moment. It doesn't have to be loud and draw attention. One can make a quiet splash or a (loud splash) if one is so inclined. Life is short. Live and let live.

Eleven
Stop apologizing; it's their fault not yours

We spend so much of our youth explaining ourselves, defending our positions and apologizing, sometimes for things we didn't even do, it's actually ridiculous, and it's the biggest time waster. Then you get to the point where you say, "wait a minute, that wasn't me and I'm not going to apologize for it." It is inevitable. It is going to happen.

I remember a few years ago, I was visiting with some folks (friends of friends) who were very religious and they happened to be Baptists. I was raised Catholic but I am not religious. I do not go to church very often. I consider myself "spiritual" rather than "religious." I don't subscribe to any monopolistic beliefs on God or spirituality. I believe God belongs to all people. Nobody has a monopoly on God and I don't care if they're Gentile, Catholic, Baptist, Buddhist, or Jewish or whatever a person happens to be. God loves us all equally. He is totally impartial.

The people I was visiting were very convicted in their religious beliefs and tried to convince me of the error or my ways as not only having been raised Catholic, but my refusal to go to church on a regular basis--and certainly, my failure to go to a Baptist church. I felt very violated in a spiritual sense because there I was trying to embrace their right to freely practice their faith the way they saw fit, but all I was getting from them was judgment about the way I went about my own spirituality, and the fact that I was raised

Catholic. After a few days, blurted, "I am not going to apologize for being raised a Catholic! I am not going to apologize for the sins of the Catholic Church! I am not Mrs. Pope! I do not even go to church! And you do not have a monopoly on God just because you can talk in alien tongues!" Well, that was the end of their hospitality. Neither they nor I could wait for me to leave after that.

It goes a lot deeper than religion. When we are young, we are unsure of ourselves and often allow others to impose their will on us. We allow others to define us. We allow others to tell us how to be, how to live, who to love, what to wear, what to study in college, where to live, who to live with, what kind of job we should aspire to have, the kind of car we should aspire to drive, and who to vote for. We allow others to judge us based on things we cannot or would not change in ourselves including our gender, race, nationality, inclinations, proclivities and culture. The thing I have come to realize is that nobody can judge me unless I give them pause. In other words, their opinion matters only matters if I allow it to matter. It only matters if somehow, I allow that person to be more important than they have a right to be in my life. It only matters if I allow myself to change in order to comport to their definition of me.

We apologize in our close relationships too, in our marriages, families, friendships and affairs. Often there is a "dominant" person in the relationship who we have allowed to call the shots. We get stuck in our roles, they as dominant; we as subservient. We find ourselves overcompensating, denying ourselves various entitlements, saying yes when we really want to say no. We do this just to keep the peace, to keep the relationship. We are afraid that if we take a stand, if we refuse to be controlled, we will lose love, we will lose that person we hold so dear in our lives.

But I beg the question, how dear is somebody in your life if they have you apologizing for things you did not do? How dear is someone if all they do is judge you? How dear is someone if they try to keep you in a box? I have heard Oprah say that she has earned her crown and she wears it without making excuses, or apologizing. This is important. At some point one has to stand up and say, this is me. This is who I am. I am not going to dim my light so that everybody around me feels better. I am going to be all that I was meant to be. And I will not apologize or self deprecate. Failure to do this means one will be left behind, always finishing last while everyone else advances themselves by climbing on one's back or shoulders. Nice girls do finish last. It doesn't pay to be too nice.

Don't get me wrong in any relationship nobody is always right. In any relationship we all, at some point, need to apologize for the wrongs we do unto each other. This is not the situation I mean. I mean those situations where you have done nothing wrong, yet someone tries to impose their will on you enough that you find yourself backing down, changing your course, apologizing. I say get rid of such a person very quick. If that's not possible, just stand firm and say, "I am not going to apologize to you for being myself. Either deal with it or scram."

If I talked to Oprah, Donald Trump and Jesus I think they would say the following:

Oprah: I've always said on this show that I was a lost soul when I was younger. I would not go back to those years, it's so much better now. I put up with so much in my youth, especially from men. I wear my crown now. I do not apologize for anything what I am, it has shaped me, it was necessary for me to go through all of that, to get here. I remember when Steadman came I was like, "what do you want?" Finally after pursuing me for months, he said he would leave me alone if that's what I wanted. I wasn't about to apologize for giving him a hard time but I wasn't about to lose this gorgeous, tall stud muffin either. I had put him to the test, and I believed that he was different. So I gave him a chance. It turns out that he was the one. With him, I live my best life. But I don't think I want to get married to him. We've been together for over twenty years and it works so why fix it when it's not broke? You know, I've decided that I won't discuss my private life on the air anymore. So that's it about me and Steadman. And I'm not going to explain or apologize for that either.

Donald Trump: They want me to apologize for so much, starting with my hair. They would love to see me apologize to certain people I blasted in my books. I will never apologize for my hair. Melania loves my comb over and she fixed Barron's comb over. And I will never apologize for outing a disloyal schmuck. I do a lot for my friends; I expect a lot back. That's how it is: Quid pro quo. That's the way it works. That is why I can never forgive that certain someone in the upper echelons of New York politics who shall remain nameless who did not quo my quid. Just know that he was supposed to be my friend and I supported him and when it was his chance to support me, he told me to take a hike. I am not going to apologize for outing him as a schmuck. He was disloyal. His wife is lovely. She deserves better than that schmuck.

That TV personality who shall remain nameless made a very big mistake. I am not going to apologize for shredding her. I tell the truth. I only say the truth. I don't believe in creating havoc without a good reason.

That Domestic Diva who shall also remain nameless made a big comeback but she never should have said what she said about me and the Apprentice. I had to set the record straight.

I don't apologize except if I forget my wife's birthday and I didn't stop in at Asprey to buy her any diamonds--and that will never happen since I stop in at Asprey all the time to buy diamonds for my wife because my wife is exquisite and should only be seen in diamonds, just like royalty. Besides, I don't want to sleep on the couch.

So, my advice is, never apologize to these vermin. Let them apologize to you. Attack them like a dog till they surrender. Don't let them get away with anything. In love, you can apologize if your wife is beautiful like my wife, but get a prenup. "Always get a prenup." Don't be stupid. This is business it's not a beauty contest. Otherwise you'll be apologizing to yourself for the bloodbath you'll swim in once love turns to hate and your wife asks for a divorce and walks away with all your money and marries George Clooney, who is short.

Jesus: If you have not sinned, there is no need to apologize. If you have sinned apologize. Amen.

When I put it all together, my grand conclusion is: Stand your ground but stop short of hurting others without a good reason; if you hurt others without cause then apologize. Mr. Trump might say that your best life means being unapologetically tough. I think it is easier on the heart to go a little softer on some people, some of the time.

Twelve
Ye are mortal

They say there are two things that are certain in life, death and taxes. I am here to tell you there is only one thing that is certain in life. And that is death. Taxes, you can find a way around with a creative accountant and the cunning to create off shore-trusts in Switzerland or the Bahamas. But you cannot wiggle your way out of death when your time is up. Not even Jesus could pull that off.

Death is a very morbid subject for most people, and it is a morbid subject for me to write about. I don't like to think about death. I am forty years old, but I still can't imagine that even I will one day croak. Oh, I know it will happen, on a philosophical level, but pragmatically, I can't even begin to picture this--although I have already instructed my family that if I go first, I want to be cremated and from a white boat, be sprinkled on a beautiful clear sunny day, over the calm aqua seas of Antigua.

What does the knowledge of my mortality do for me other than scare me? Well, it makes me want to hurry up and get things accomplished in my life, to stop wasting time. There is so much more I can do, and should do. I want to leave something behind, to be remembered. I want to contribute to society. I want to be a good parent. I want to sit with Oprah Winfrey on her show and discuss my New York Times best-selling book. I want to visit the White House. I want to have a successful law practice. I want to make at least one million dollars from my work. I want to buy a house in the Hamptons. I want a dog who I'll name Happy.

There is so much my mortality teaches me. First of all, it cautions me to stop taking life for granted. It commands that I safeguard my health. It commands that I do what my conscience says is right, and refrain from doing what it tells me is wrong. It commands that I remain humble, that I don't allow myself to get too big for my britches no matter what is going on in my life, or how much I think I have. It tells me that my mere mortality makes me equal, not more or less than any other human being. It commands that I don't waste time on emotions like depression, anger and envy. These can eat up good years which are so precious. It commands that I stay focused on achieving the goals I have set for myself. It commands that I express my gratitude for being here, and for the things I have. It commands that I do not fear death but rather see it as just another part of this beautiful life. It commands that I find happiness, peace and joy in whatever the circumstances that I find myself. It commands that I be all I can be when I still have the chance.

If I talked to Oprah, Donald Trump and Jesus I think they would say the following:

Oprah: Live your best life while you still can!

Donald Trump: You're here today gone tomorrow. Nobody cares. You're on your own. Do everything you possibly can. *Think Big and Kick Ass.* I'm telling you there's no other way. Oh, and by the way, when you kick ass make sure to use your left foot. Believe me there's a scientific reason for this which I will disclose in my next memoir.

Jesus: Follow the commandments and you will be immortal. Love God, Love thy neighbor. Treat thy body as a temple and thou shalt live forever. Amen.

When I put it all together my grand conclusion is: While you have life, do the best you can to live as well as you can; but live a life of love—for others and for yourself; and while you're at it, kick some ass too.

Thirteen

Who cares what everybody else is doing?

You live as long as I have, you begin to realize how irrelevant it is what other people are doing with their lives and how pointless it is to try to keep up with anybody else. There are always going to be greater and lesser persons than yourself who are ahead or behind you in some way, shape or form. Keep up with yourself. It is only important what you are doing, and what the quality of life you are creating for yourself. Be yourself. Mind your business. Who cares what everybody else is doing? Why focus on it? Just do your own thing.

Maybe I am being disingenuous. How can I say this with a straight face and turn around and call myself a late bloomer? If I am a late bloomer it means there is a benchmark—someone I am looking to as the ideal, right? It means I am comparing myself to others and I've concluded that I am coming up short—hence the "late" bloom. This is very hypocritical of me. I'll tell you something: I don't like this. I don't want to compare myself to anybody else anymore. Why should I concern myself with how many other forty year olds are leading perfect, productive lives with perfect mates and perfect kids and perfect jobs which pay them big bucks all of which they save on their prodigious bank accounts? I am not them. And the only thing it does for me by focusing on them is frustrate me and make me feel like a loser. Obviously nobody is an island. To some extent, we look to each other for inspiration, guidance and a reality check. That's fine. But it has to be kept in perspective.

Is it that we are all like flowers? Is there a right time and month and year to bloom? Or is this notion passé? Who says you have to have kids before forty? Who says your career has to be totally developed by forty? Who says you have to get married by forty? Who says you have to own real estate by forty? Who says you have to have all this sexual experience at forty? Who says you should "look" forty? What does that even mean? Who says you can't feel more comfortable in jeans than a suit at forty? Who says you are in mid-life at forty? What if you live to 100? Then you are not going to be in your mid-life for another ten years! It would also mean you have sixty more years to figure things out—which is an eternity from my perspective. It means if you get married at forty and both of you lived to be 90 you would celebrate your 50th anniversary which is a heck of a long time. Who says forty is this magical midpoint where you have to have it all together or else? I am not suggesting that forty is nothing. It's a big age. It's significant. But maybe its not as fatal as some of us think it is. In fact, this whole mid-life at forty thing seems so arbitrary now that I think about it. And it's too much unnecessary pressure.

So hush. Don't panic. You will be fine. Just get into kinetic mode. Stop being such a huge potential. Act. Do something. Create something. Don't just sit there staring at your "mid-life" and having a crisis cause nothing makes sense. Get up. Get off your butt and do something about your life! Turn that mid-life, late blooming crisis on its nose. Sure it's a Sisyphean task; but take a cue from people like Oprah, Donald Trump and Jesus. If they are not proof that more is possible, then there is no proof. But set your own pace. Compete with yourself. If your pace is too slow for you, speed up. If your pace is fine for you, don't change it. If your pace is too fast for you, slow down. Don't measure yourself using anybody else's measuring stick. Aren't you too old to be dictated to in this manner any more? You will bloom when you are ready, not before. Flowers have to be left alone to bloom when they are ready to bloom. If you force it, you could kill the flower.

If I talked to Oprah, Donald Trump and Jesus I think they would say the following:

Oprah: I am a total believer in living your own best life. At the risk of repeating myself, I think it's worth repeating: Live *your* best life. Not everybody else's best life.   Everybody can't be Oprah Winfrey. I don't say that to be conceited. It's just the way it is.   Live your best life. Don't compete with or aspire to be anybody else.

Donald Trump: I'm a very competitive guy. I compete with myself because I always want to be better. I always want to be the best. But I compete with my peers too. You can call it friendly competition. It's not that I care what they are doing. But we compete. We even compete on the golf course. On my show the Apprentice, it's all about competition. Every body wants to be the best but only one person will ultimately triumph. I always want to be the best. I want the best buildings, I want the best Vodka, and I want the best spouse. I want the best steak. I want the best golf courses. That's just my M.O. I can't be anybody else. Do I enjoy competing? Of course. I remember one time Steve Wynn and I were competing for a Vegas deal. Steve is my good friend and I love him. But the best man won that competition. That was me. Competition is business. You can't be the best if you don't compete. In my line of business, I always have one contractor competing with another; I have banks competing with banks; I have lawyers competing with lawyers. Competition is economical. It's about the economy, stupid.

Jesus: If you must imitate another, let it be God. Amen.

When I put it all together, my grand conclusion is: you can only live *your* best life. Competition could be overrated if it is taken to an extreme. Sure it fuels business but life is not all business. Life is not "the Apprentice." Life is not competitive golf. Look, would I be the worse soccer mom if I ever had kids? Of course. But it doesn't make it right and it doesn't make it fulfilling. Our best lives is a happy dose of balance, abundance, consideration for others, love for ourselves and a spiritual connection.

Fourteen

Worry about yourself yet give a fig about what is going on in the world

By the time you read this, Hillary Clinton will probably be President, or have suffered one of the biggest upsets in American political history. In which case, Either Barrack Obama or Michael Bloomberg, or some other guy will probably be sitting in the Oval Office. Any way this cake gets sliced, it's sure to be interesting. For me, if Hilary or Obama wins, it's win win: Hilary because she's a smart woman; Obama because he is a smart man. Either way the next four years will be interesting. I can fantasize about getting invited to the White House if it's one of those two

I never used to care about who was president. I never used to vote even when I had the legal right to do so. I used to feel that my vote would not make a difference. I used to feel that it was no skin off my back whoever was living in the White House. I don't feel that way anymore. Each of us is responsible for our environment, society, neighborhood, country and world. Just like we create our lives and sculpt our lives, we sculpt our world, we create our countries. The world we create and sculpt has ripple effects on the quality of our lives; it is handed down to our progeny whose job will be so much more difficult if what we pass down to them is crap.

Right now, there is a lot of crap that is going on in our world. Not just in our country.

I read on the internet that young people don't listen to the news as much as they used to generations ago. They do not buy as many newspapers. They don't vote. I am not surprised. I was one of those young people. I did not give a fig. If it didn't affect me directly, why should I worry my head? I had enough problems in my immediate life. I did not need to worry about what was going on in the world.

But you know what I am discovering? Michael Jackson was totally right when he said: "We are the World!" Don't laugh, I'm being serious. Each of us, individually and collectively, is the world. There is no world, without the people. There are no people without each individual person. There's only one world. Each person is responsible in some small way for the world. It matters what is happening. It matters what we do, and what we don't do. It is not enough to say we have enough to eat, therefore let others worry about themselves. It is not enough to say we are "free" so let others free themselves however they can. But that is not to say we impose our will on others. It's a very fine line. Everyone does not have to be a Democrat. Everyone does not have to practice Democracy. People must be free to live in the way they choose, but there is a line that has to be drawn. There is a price that has to be paid. And that is why, to some extent, we all have to police each other. Because we all pay the price in the end.

We are a part of a divine creation of interconnectivity. We are not an island. We can never be. A person who is an island is a person who is marked for extinction. If humanity is to continue to exist, each human being has to care about humanity's existence and actively seek, in whatever small way, to preserve it. Our survival depends on the survival of other fellow humans. Our health depends on the health of others. Our peace depends on the peace of others. Our justice depends on whether there is justice for others. Sure, I think our first responsibility is ourselves. It is human to be selfish. Selflessness is hypocrisy on steroids. Nobody is truly selfless. But after that, we have to give a fig about others, and about the world. We have to do whatever small feats we can to contribute to our world, even if it's just taking shorter showers to save water, or voting for leaders who also give a fig. It matters who we (the people of the world) elect into government. It matters that people are free to elect their government. It matters what is going on in other countries in the world. We have to care because ultimately, it will affect us.

When people get fed up and sick and tired of the status quo and they feel like nobody cares and nobody is listening, they do desperate things that affects us all. What affects the few affects the masses--in the end.

Fight this truth all you want but it is futility.

If I talked to Oprah, Donald Trump and Jesus I think they would say the following:

Oprah: We have to care. We have to give a fig about each other. That is what it is about. That is why I continue to do the work I do. If I didn't give a fig I would stop doing Oprah shows. I certainly don't do it for the money. I do it because I care about people living their best lives.

Donald Trump: I am the biggest philanthropist in real estate. I am a very generous business man. But I am not an idiot. I don't go around throwing money away. I give millions of dollars to so many causes. They call me for money and I write the checks--if I believe in the cause. I am not a chump. I did the rink in Central Park because I love New York and I love people. I give a fig. I allow injured vets to stay at my home in Palm Beach every year. Why? Because I give a fig. I employ thousands of people in my casinos and all my other businesses around the world. But I want employees who give a fig about me. That is why I fired Carolyn Kepcher. She stopped giving a fig about my business. And I stopped giving a fig about her need for a high profile job.

Jesus: Give a fig. Amen.

When I put it all together, my grand conclusion is: One ought to find a cause to care about and do it. One ought to give a fig. It doesn't have to be huge. Maybe we can start by not wasting so much paper. Or taking shorter showers. Or carpooling sometimes.

No Frogs Please

Fifteen
Infatuation is folly

Choose a partner wisely. A wrong choice can be dire. A wrong choice wastes a lot of precious time. Just because you may have been with someone till time immemorial does not mean that he or she is the right mate for you (although if it has been more than twenty years you might as well stick with and forget it.) But for the rest of us, just because you may fancy yourself in love with every Tommy, Dickey and Harry who flashes you a sexy grin, does not mean that it would make sense to be with, or get involved with said person. Because if you are not all you can be with someone, if you feel you cannot "blossom into more" because of the person you are with, I am here to suggest that this may not the right person for you.

In youth, it is often very difficult to make these distinctions. Physical attraction and infatuation are so often mistaken for love. Love is serious business. It is grave. It can only come from knowing someone. It can only come where there is trust and mutual respect. Love never ends. And it is two-sided. It is a magnetic thing. If you're "madly head over heels in love with this guy," and he's treating you like crap, and you're still "madly head over heels in love," something is wrong. It's not love. Love is magnetic. True love is magnetic. What you're probably experiencing is masochism. And it's going to hurt. It's going to hurt badly. You're going to be on the floor grabbing on to his ankles begging him not to go and he's going to drag you sorry behind to the door and he's going to open the door and leave you there lying on your stomach on the floor, and walk away without looking back. And there you will be. But with time, you will start to see through the glass clearly.

I am finally at the point now where I realize that it is imperative that I only allow myself indulgences—including those mental affairs I am so skilled at—that pays a dividend. By that I mean, unless there is something in this entanglement that can impact my life in a good way, don't get involved. As far as men are concerned, it is crystal clear now that I must only associate with men who are ready, willing and able to be an "appropriate mate" for me, even in, especially in, my mind. Otherwise, it's a total waste of time and energy. It is a waste of my thoughts. I am better off alone in that case.

The price of sticking to this resolve is high. It could mean never finding Mr. Right. In which case, the price of only allowing an "appropriate" man into my orbit could be very high. But I think it's more economical than the alternative.

You see, "thoughts have wings." "Thoughts are things." "Thoughts manifest." Fantasizing about a man who at the outset has other responsibilities and distractions that involve other women, work, past times and proclivities means that I am taking the chance that I could one day end up being involved with him in spite of his wrongness for me and all I will be is a second class mistress, at best. I would be saddling myself with an inappropriate liability, not an asset; robbing myself of getting any dividends from the investment of my time, energy, and "love." What will be the result of this investment? My dividends will be misery, of course. I will jeopardize my emotional equilibrium and this in turn will have ripple effects in my life, including my professional life and my spiritual life. There is no bigger screw up than saddling oneself with the wrong mate, boyfriend, significant other, and "mental" Romeo. That can set you back years. That can really destroy any progress you have made in your life--and it's so hard to rebound, to get back to neutral.

Being 40 is great because a woman starts to understand with perfect clarity that she is the "architect of her own life." She sculpts everything that her life is. If her life is crappy, she sculpted the crap. It is her choice to get involved with an obvious Mr. Wrong, or not. It is her responsibility to pay attention to what a man is saying both with his verbal and nonverbal communication--and mostly the nonverbal which is mostly how men speak. She owes herself that duty of care. She is held to the task of allowing only a decent, kind, loving and "appropriate" man into her orbit and if it means never finding him and remaining single for the rest of her life, so it shall be written; and so it shall be done. She will not settle for anything less.

She accepts that she cannot depend on anybody else to save her from her own bad judgment. She cannot continue to turn a blind eye like she has been known to do in the past, and ignore red flags, and practice this tiresome naiveté some of us practice so well, and fail to watch her back for scoundrels and infidels who have the power to blow her best laid plan to smithereens in no time flat--with lies and empty promises that any fool should have seen for what it was. This is just too juvenile to be excused at this juncture in her life. It is simple: a woman of forty knows that if she wants dividends, she has to make good investments. She can't just fling her hard earned assets wherever they will land and hope for the best. That kind of folly is a sin at this stage in the game.

If I talked to Oprah, Donald Trump and Jesus I think they would say the following:

Oprah: What can I say? When you're young and dumb you're young and dumb. That's why I've done all these Oprah Winfrey Shows about this subject. But no matter how many shows I do, there are going to be a lot of people who can only learn from their own mistakes. I say, if you make a mistake, move on. Don't dwell on the past. Live your best life now!

Donald: Big laugh. Then he shakes his head and says, "Look at least I know who to handle pressure."

Jesus: The Lord thy God does not condone fornication. Blessed is he who does not infatuate, fornicate or adulterate. The Lord thy God gave us three things: Hope, Faith and love. The greatest of these is Love. Blessed be God. Blessed be his Holy Name. Amen.

When I put it all together my grand conclusion is: Be careful in the choices you make. Love is too important to be treated lightly.

Sixteen
Be thankful for your vajajay (or whatever you have)

Oprah was the first person who glamorized gratitude when she started her gratitude journal advocacy in the late eighties or early nineties. Even movie icons like Gwyneth Paltrow got in on the act and I remember her telling Oprah that she too kept a journal. I was absolutely amazed by that. I thought, "Wow, even Gwyneth takes the time to fill a gratitude journal?" I used to keep a journal too. But then, as time went on, I stopped. I just got too busy. But lately, I started to write down the things I am grateful for, not on a daily basis, but as often as I can. However, I try not to let a day go by without making oral declarations of my gratitude. For example, I write daily lists of things to do, and I always list "give thanks" as one of the things to do. So I will be in my office with the lights dimmed and I will literally take time out to give thanks for all my blessings. It's funny because I used to think I had nothing, so how could I keep a gratitude journal, how can I give thanks? I realize now that I have so much, especially when I start to say all the things I am thankful for. It is almost an infinite list of things.

I am here to tell you that if you are breathing, that's already a thousand things to be thankful for. If you're forty and you're breathing, that is not nothing either. And even if you're dead, you should probably be thankful for that too because at least you know you won't have to pay any more taxes. We all can find at least twenty things to be thankful for every single day. I am going to rattle off forty things right now. I am thankful for my eyes. I am thankful for my hands. I am thankful for my ears. I am thankful for my tongue. I am thankful for my nose. I am thankful for my legs. I am thankful for my feet. I am thankful for my knees. I am thankful for my heart. I am thankful for my intestines.

I am thankful for my butt. *I am thankful for my vajayjay and I vow to protect her from all miscreants from now on!* I am thankful for my fingers. I am thankful for my hair. I am thankful for my ovaries and my eggs. I am thankful for my period. I am thankful for my uterus. I am thankful for my breasts. I am thankful for my teeth. I am thankful for my brain. I am thankful for my imagination. I am thankful for my creativity. I am thankful for my ability to laugh. I am thankful for anyone who makes me laugh. I am thankful for my family. I am thankful for my mother. I am thankful for my father. I am thankful for my sisters. I am thankful for my brother. I am thankful for my nieces. I am thankful for my nephews. I am thankful for my aunts and uncles and my grandmothers and my cousins. I am thankful for my work. I am thankful for my clients. I am thankful for the money my clients pay to me that allows me to live. I am thankful for my colleagues that I can ask a question when I am in a jam.

I am thankful for all the other writers in the world who inspire my own writing...did I name forty things yet? I am thankful for Oprah and Donald Trump because they prove that more is possible. I am thankful for the fact that I am a citizen of the United States. I am thankful for the fact that I was born in Antigua. I want to embody the best of both worlds.

I am thankful for my health. I am thankful for my health. I am thankful for my health. I am thankful that I have enough to eat. I am thankful that I have a roof over my head. I am thankful that I can hold my cat and listen to him purr. I am thankful for the air I breathe. I am thankful for the sun I can feel and see. I am thankful for the snow I can ski in although I don't know how to ski. I am thankful for grass and trees. I am thankful for whoever invented marshmallows. I am thankful for Greyhound buses. I am thankful for people who still believe we can achieve world peace. I am thankful for fruit of the loom underwear. I am thankful that I can get a breast lift if I choose because I'm definitely going to need one since, as my grandmother would say, "the necks of my breasts are broken."

I think when we take the time out of our busy lives to dwell on the things we have, especially those things we take for granted, we realize how blessed we really are. Because, saying I am grateful for my eyes seems so intuitive, but there are so many people who can't see. Saying I am grateful for my knees seem silly, but so many people are at the hospital right now getting knee replacement surgery. Being grateful for my ovaries and eggs and my period is a big deal cause I am a forty year old broad who still dreams of having a biological child. And I am thankful to the max for my vajayjay because I just wouldn't know what to do with a penis.

If I talked to Oprah, Donald Trump and Jesus I think they would say the following:

Oprah: I love my vajayjay! Ladies, let's talk about our vajayjays! Let's live our best life! I've done at least 10,000 Oprah shows over the years. But this is my favorite! Free copies of the book: *The anatomy of the vajayjay: how to care for and calm your vajayjay and protect her all from miscreants!* by Anonymous, for every audience member! Long live the vajayjay! There are only five men in the audience today! (Says Oprah to the man nearest to her microphone)

"Sir, don't you love your wife's vajajay? (Says the man) "Actually, I'm not married. I'm here with my boyfriend."

Donald Trump: I am a simple guy from Queens and I have partaken of some amazing vajayjays belonging to some of the most famous, beautiful, perfumed and spectacular women in the World! There's nothing like a good vajayjay. Each of my wives is a spectacular woman. Ivana is spectacular. Marla is spectacular. Melania is spectacular. Sometimes I had to pinch myself to make sure I wasn't dreaming. If you only knew the vajayjays I have seen! I would tell you, but I don't want to create havoc.

Jesus: The father in Heaven created Adam and Eve in the Garden of Eden. Eve was tempted by the serpent. Suddenly, she became aware of her vajayjay. It was not the plan of the Father that Eve would be aware of her vajajay, but in all things, give thanks to the Almighty God, for because of Eve, all women are aware of their vajayjays and all men are similarly aware of women's vajayjays. Blessed be the name of the Lord. Halleluiah. Amen.

When I put it all together my grand conclusion is: A vajayjay is a priced possession.

Seventeen
Don't settle for a frog

Just today, two full weeks into my new decade, I read a book about turning forty and in it the author said, "71% of forty year old own their own homes, 51% are happy, 91% of women have been married and 82% have had children." Whereas I had figured I was a late bloomer before, now I know that I must have really screwed up big time if I can't answer in the affirmative to anything, whatsoever, that a normal 40 year old should have done. I tell you I could barely focus enough to write after I read that book. I just wanted to curl up and die.

Well obviously I have to pull myself together. I have to fix my head, rethink my situation, put a spin on it or I will lose my mind. What is the spin I can put on this mess? Oh, and the author also said, "forty year olds are 'getting it on' 1.8 times per week." Oh My God.

The thing that scares me the most is the fact that until I read the book I totally didn't realize that I'm not like normal people. I was living in my own little bubble where I didn't have to worry about much, including shaving my legs and wearing sexy underwear and all those tedious stuff. I like wearing my granny panties (navel knockers as we call them in the Old Country); quite frankly they make me laugh when I get dressed in the mornings and one of them hits my rib cage.

It's just that I got tired of kissing frogs so I shut down, you know? I gave up on finding my prince. I know that I should not allow the frogs I've kissed to completely destroy my faith in every member of the opposite sex. I owe it to myself not to. Even if I never find Him, it should not be because I gave up looking. If I don't find a way to reconcile my bad judgment and disillusionment with men in the past, I may, if I am not careful, end up my whole life alone. And I love my own company, don't get me wrong. I am not one of those women who have to have a man in order to feel whole. I can take care of myself. My happiness and my joy are my job. I handle my job as well as I can. But there are distinct times when a woman wants a partner to share her life. And ain't I a woman? That is not to say I am going to settle. I will not settle. Not even if it means spinsterhood forever and navel knockers that cover my breasts. I will not settle. But I should at least try making eye contact. And maybe I should put an ad on E-Harmony and Match.com. And maybe I should go browse in Victoria's Secret. The only thing I worry about is how can I tell when a guy is on the "down low"? This thought makes me tense.

If I talked to Oprah, Donald Trump and Jesus I think they would say the following:

Oprah: If I told you all the mistakes I made in my life you wouldn't believe it. But I have moved on. If I dwelled on past screw ups I wouldn't be able to do what I've done. In order to live your best life, you have to make peace with the fact that you are not perfect. You are mortal. Mistakes are a part of the experience. I made so many mistakes, I kissed many frogs; and then I found Steadman. If I had given up on men, I would never have found Steadman.

Donald: I don't date frogs and you shouldn't either. I am a prince and every one of my exes will tell you that. In the nineties I made big mistakes when I was focused on supermodels and not on my bottom line. I got sloppy and my business nearly collapsed. I made mistakes in my marriages too. I have learned that when you're married, dating other women doesn't "go over big with your wife." I make peace with that because I learned from my "wrong-headedness." You can't take your wife and someone else on a ski trip. That is just dumb and wrongheaded. You cannot focus when you do that. I learned that you have to stay focused at all times. You cannot afford to lose focus by thinking of the past. Think of the present and the future. Never obsess about the past. Make peace with it and move on. Look at Omarosa. It's not that she was a frog but she moved on from her disastrous performance on the

Apprentice. She got her breasts enhanced surgically; she went on a few more shows. Then she came back to the Apprentice as a celebrity. She did Celebrity Apprentice. Because she made peace with her past screw ups and I forgave her. She became the female equivalent of a prince. People think I forgave her to get ratings. But in fact, I forgave her because she was truly sorry for being too big for her britches on the first Apprentice. And she humbled herself. This is the sign of a great individual. Now she and I are friends. But I would never hire her. Never is too soon, actually.

Jesus: And ye shall find. But be specific. Amen.

When I put it all together my grand conclusion is: Never piss off Mr. Trump. And never give up hope. Things can change. All you have to do is seek change and it will happen. But be specific about the kind of change you are seeking.

Eighteen
The Breast Lift (to do it or not to do it?)

Hollywood has glamorized plastic surgery like nobody's business. So many procedures and so little time! One can get a face lift, breast lift, butt lift and chin lift. One can rearrange one's nose, lips, eyes and thighs. One can suction out one's fatty deposits in the waist. One can even reconfigure one's privates. It's amazing. It's hard to find anyone in Hollywood except maybe for Nicole Kidman and Oprah, who never had anything done. I look at Joan Rivers, Janice Dickson, Kathy Lee Gifford, Pamela Anderson, Posh Spice and Michael Jackson and I am awed by the lengths people will go, and can go, to achieve the ideal face and beauty. To go under the knife, or not to go under the knife? That is the question.

The truth of the matter is I am not as hot as I used to be. As the years progress, I know I will get colder and colder in the looks department unless I do something to arrest Mother Nature. But what? Could I really ever go under the knife to turn back Time? I'm just not sure. I mean, it's all good if an individual wants this and I think certainly nobody has the right to tell a forty year old woman who's just starting to see her looks begin to fade to "grow old gracefully" if she feels she can improve her looks with a surgeon's scalpel. But plastic surgery is definitely not for everybody. Oh, it seems glamorous and easy and quick and accessible. But I am not fully convinced that things are as they seem with this. Surgery to me--any surgery--is serious. All I can think of when I think of getting cut up is, needing a blood transfusion when I'm done. I really want to avoid having to do that at all costs. Look what happened to Kanye's mother. And Star Jones. She apparently needed a blood transfusion after she got her breasts done (apparently being the operative word here.)

To be perfectly frank, I don't really care who's done what and why they have done it. What I care about is the fact that I'm going green, and I think these "plastics" used for surgical enhancements may have toxic chemicals in them which could be hazardous to one's health. And because it's a relatively new "movement" nobody will realize it for another twenty years, at which point so many people would have developed so many ailments. Even if I am being ridiculous and these "plastics" or perfectly safe, I am not altogether sure I want to reconfigure my body parts all in the name of having lips like Angelina, a booty like Beyonce and tits like Pamela Anderson. Does it upset God, I wonder?

When I was twenty years old, I was working at a rectory on Midagh Street in Brooklyn Heights and one night a young woman and two young men came to buy a Mass Card. She was more beautiful than Halle Berry and I thought the guys she was with were her friends. I figured them to be about my age. Upon further inquiry, however, it turns out that this woman was forty years old and one man was her husband and the other was their twenty year old son! I could not believe it. I asked her "what was the secret to her youthfulness?" She said happiness, and never badmouthing anybody. But, she cautioned, "don't be too impressed. I have forty year old breasts." For the life of me, I could not fathom what that could look like. But it sounded ominous. My own breasts, only twenty years old, were racked, stacked, and perfectly saluting the sun, hallelujah! What possibly could forty year old breasts look like? It boggled my mind. She said, "don't worry, you'll find out soon enough. "I'm here to tell you that forty year old breasts have a definite look. It is called s.c.a.r.y. (As my grandmother, Claudina, would say in dialect: "dem neck bruck." Translation: their necks are broken.) Would I ever get them done? I don't know. I still can't take a position. Do me a favor. Ask me about this one when I'm forty-five.

If I talked to Oprah, Donald Trump and Jesus I think they would say the following:

Oprah: Let's talk about breasts with broken necks. I'll tell you something, sometimes I feel like I have to fold up my breasts; I wonder, what happened to my breasts?! But I would never get them done. I want to live my best life, and so should you, so if I change my mind and decide to get em done, I will tell you.

Donald Trump: As a general rule I think it is vulgar to discuss women's body parts. But I will say this: I believe in plastic surgery. I am for it. A woman's job is to be beautiful. My job is to make money. Believe me, I know about this stuff. I could never have a wife whose breasts have broken necks. All my wives had spectacular breasts.

Jesus: The flesh is just flesh. It does not matter how it looks, it is still flesh. Do not be controlled by the flesh and the things of it. Ye are dead. Amen.

When I put it all together my grand conclusion is: Breasts are just flesh; but they do look a lot better when they are surgically enhanced and today's men seem to go for gravity-defying fake ones than sagging real ones. Oprah is rich enough that she doesn't care what anybody thinks about her breasts. If we were all as rich as Oprah, we wouldn't have to think about lifting our breasts.

Nineteen
Cellulite, grey hairs, chins hairs

Whose dimply butt *is* this? Not mine. I have no butt dimples thank God. But I am starting to get gray hairs on my head! Where are these gray hairs coming from?! Luckily I can still use tweezers to pluck them out. It is not necessary to color them yet. One of my friends once told me that if she tweezed her grays out like I did, she would be bald. That's because she's gray all over. I don't want to think about being gray all over. It is traumatic enough to have to pluck the gray strands from the side of my head. I did not have to do this at thirty. Ten years does make a very big difference. What can I eat to arrest this problem?

Oh, and if that's not bad enough, why do I suddenly have to pluck my chin? I used to hear Oprah talk about her "beard" and she would have a good laugh. And I would laugh too. But it wasn't funny when I saw a random hair follicle had sprung up on my own jaw. That was not funny at all. When I was a little girl, I remember seeing my grandmother, Dovie, picking relentlessly at her chin. In those days she did not have tweezers and would always be picking at her chin as if she were a woodpecker. "Granny, what are you doing?" I would ask. She would respond in dialect, "*tek time gee-al. Pig min ask e mouma wa mek e mouth so lang. She tell e tek time picknie u will fine out.*" Translate: A pig asked her mother, why is your mouth so long? She told him, take your time, child, you will find out." Today, I find myself picking at my chin as if I were woodpecker.

As far as the cellulite, this is deceiving because I think people think only over the hill women get it, but I am here to tell you that I have skinny young pals who have cellulite--a lot of it too and they are well under forty. I have seen movie stars parading the beaches of Hawaii and the Caribbean and sporting dimples in their thighs and sometimes in their butts if they are brave enough to wear a thong.

I think cellulite is a great insult to womankind. It is cruel and unusual punishment too. It could seriously prevent a woman from getting a husband, a task which is already a damn near impossibility if she is forty and never tied the knot. How could nature have done this to perfectly good women? It is so mean to turn a woman into a dimply, uneven alligator-skinned nightmare when she just as easily could age as gracefully as a man. Men age with such grace. They do not get cellulite. They look distinguished with gray hair. They look sexy with a beard. They can find a young wife even if they are one foot out of the grave at the tender age of 96. And they can sire kids till the end of time. It hardly seems fair.

If I talked to Oprah, Donald Trump and Jesus I think they would say the following:

Oprah: Just get a private chef and live your best life. I hear that drinking a lot of coffee reduces cellulite. As for the beard, Steadman teases me about that all the time. Everybody knows I get facial hair on my chin. So what? Pluck em and move on. There are so many other important things.

Donald Trump: I am over sixty and I am still able to procreate myself. I am still fertile. "I can still produce kids." It's sweet. It's as it should be. Two of my wives probably can no longer produce kids. But it is different for men. I can always produce kids. You should see my latest. He is a joy. I love to hold him and kiss him at five in the morning when I wake up to read all the financial news for the day. But I've got to say something unpopular. And that is, facial hair on my spouse would probably be grounds for an annulment. I do not want any excess fat or hair on my spouse especially if the hair is under the chin. I am a very traditional guy. I love beautiful women. A beautiful woman does not have a beard. She does not have cellulite. She is not fat and she does not have gray hair. Look, I could care less about my appearance and *I* cover my gray. Why would I be with a woman who walked around showing her gray?

That's just disgusting. But to grow a beard and come to bed like that? DIVORCE.

Jesus: When you get to the Great White Way, ask Eve about it and she will tell you why the Father dealt women such a tough blow. Amen.

When I put it all together my grand conclusion is: It's tough to be a woman. But studies show that more men get sex change operations to become women than the other way around; so, it must also be more fun to be a woman, in spite of the challenges.

Twenty
Slay the "Mongoose"

We are animals; that is what we are. Some of us are wildebeests. Some of us are lions. Some of us are elephants. Some of us are ox. Some of us are fish. Some of us are mice. Some of us are dinosaurs. Some of us are mongooses. But we are all animals. This cannot be sugarcoated. If we are not careful, if we are not tough, if we are not strong, we will get taken down (devoured!) by bigger, stronger animals in the jungle. Each of us is prey to someone else at one time or the other. I have been prey more times than I care to admit. After so many years of perfecting my craft (of being prey) I feel sometimes, that I am no longer whole, I am just a torso. So many people have taken a bite out of me. But I am aware that if I don't put a stop to the carnage, soon, all I will be is a head--if that much.

There is a man I call Mongoose. I allowed myself to be the most pathetic prey to him. He wasn't even all that good looking in retrospect. He, in fact, resembles a mongoose in deed, and in visage. And he was a boastful, shallow cheat, to bout, so I don't know how I came to fall for his treachery. But fall I did. I am going to spare you the sordid, boring details; but suffice to say that in the last few months of our "friendship" the Mongoose and I started a company together for which he opened an office on Wall Street. The minute it seemed that the company might actually become something viable he kicked me to the curb and brought in a bunch of big wigs. I was in shock. I never dreamt he could or would do that to me. I thought

I was valued. I thought he needed me. I thought he loved me. But I should have known better. Trust me there is no excuse for my idiocy. I deserve all I got for my stupidity.

These big shot geniuses from some of the nation's top schools to came in and advised him and I was basically told, "Stay if you want to stay, go if you want to go." It was tough. But I had no choice. I could not allow myself to stay with someone who was "such a priority in my life (too funny) when I was just an option in his." So I left. I ran away to Paris.

But hush. It turns out the geniuses advised the Mongoose to tie up his town house in a Tony part of town, in the business; to personally guarantee the bank loans he took out to "grow" the business. I had advised him to do the opposite and had even formed a limited liability company so that he could protect his house. So while I was in Paris hungry and walking around the Seine trying to figure out how I could have been such an idiot, he was in New York (on Wall Street) blowing through three million dollars which he got from the bank and for which he had put his home up as collateral. His genius friends were with him enjoying the ride. They threw corporate bashes, sponsored car shows in the Hamptons, dined like royalty.

About a month ago, Mongoose chirped me on my cell phone. It was a few weeks before my 40th birthday. He wanted to invite me out Southhampton. He was renting a place there and he needed to see me. The company had collapsed. He was in danger of losing his house. He needed to "commiserate" and see how "we" could solve the problems that "he" was having. Can you believe this shit? First of all, the last time I checked, in order to "commiserate" it means that we would *both* have to be having problems.

But even assuming my life was a disaster (which between you and me it was) he was never someone who wanted to hear anything about my life, fears and problems. It was always all about him. All he wanted from me was to be there to listen to him and act as his unpaid shrink (among other things) while he burdened me with all his problems and picked my brain for solutions and left me depleted when he was done. Now here he was, back for an encore nearly seven years to the day. Can you believe this son of a gun would think that at almost forty years of age, he could pull one over me the way he did when I was 32? He had the audacity to think my life hadn't gone on, that I hadn't grown, that I hadn't learned my lesson the first time around.

It is not printable what I told him.

There have so many other ways and times that I have allowed myself to be prey. But I am at an age, thank God, where I am more aware of scavengers and I am refusing to be caught up in their ruse. It is not always "lovers." It could be friends, bosses, employees, strangers, anybody. The point is, in order to survive and to thrive, one has to be aware and one has to be strong. Do not allow everybody to come and take a bite out of you without at least a good fight. They will take everything if you let them: your heart, mind, soul, strength, energy, body, intellect, ideas, will and everything else. And what's in it for you? Zero. All it does is set you backwards. All it does is it keeps you down. All it does is waste your precious time and energy. Wasted time and energy can never be recalled. That is the lesson I have learned. There is no merciful scavenger. It is up to each person to refuse to be prey.

If I talked to Oprah, Donald Trump and Jesus I think they would say the following:

Oprah: It's very hard to live your best life if you are busy being somebody's prey. I've been there. I know how that is. But it's so not worth it. It is so avoidable too. I wish I could go back and avoid all those times I allowed myself to be prey.

Donald Trump: We are all animals. I have always said so. Nobody wants the best for anybody. Don't trust anybody. You're a fool if you think anybody wishes you the best. You are either scavenger or you are prey. You have to choose.

Jesus: Not one of ye is good. Amen.

When I put it all together my grand conclusion is: Wear Camouflage.

Find your own comfort zone

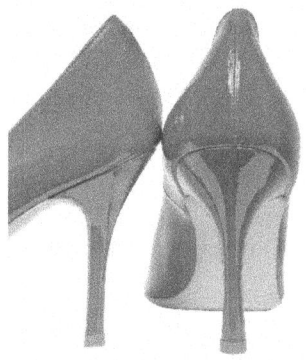

Twenty-one
How to choose a friend

My grand folks always said "you are the friends you keep." It is important to keep the right friends. Their influence can be far-reaching. "Friends" can help you advance your life and they can also keep you from advancing. One has to be careful. Not everybody how acts like a friend is a friend. Not everyone is a good influence for you. Not everyone can enable you to "live your best life." Friends should allow access to things that are good for you. If through your friends you routinely gain access to things that are not good for you, dump those friends.

Friends should be people you are not only comfortable with, but people who are comfortable with you. This is an important lesson I have learned at my not so tender age. Having friends, good friends, is important in life. Friends can come in all shapes and sizes. What matters is that your friends fit your lifestyle on some basic level and you fit theirs. I think it is folly, if, say, you are a nonsmoker, to associate only with smokers as friends. And I am totally using smoking as a parable. It could be something else that just isn't good for you. Eventually, if you hang out with people who are chain smokers and you don't smoke, you are going to start smoking, or you will still get lung cancer from all that second hand smoke, even if you don't actually put the cigarette in your mouth

Friends should share one's basic sensibilities. If not, there is bound to be uncomfortableness or problems. That is a dead give away that you are not among friends, when you can't be yourself around a person, when you are uncomfortable, or there are always problems. Be that as it may, in many significant ways, it is the differences that our friends bring to the table that adds so much zest to life that spices up our lives. We all need people we can share a good laugh with; people who bring out the best in us. This is our basic nature as human beings to need each other.

In a way friends are even more significant than family. Your family is your family and you are stuck with them no matter what. A lot of times you will find people who have family members they can't stand and vice versa. But your friends chose you and you chose them. Your friends had a choice to be friends with you or not and they chose to be friends with you and you them. Nobody has a true "friend" that they can't stand or who can't stand them. That's totally incongruous.

What would Oprah, Donald Trump and Jesus say about choosing friends?

Oprah: Everybody knows I have a best friend named Gayle. We have been friends since we did news in Chicago many moons ago. Our friendship has only intensified over the years. People accuse me and Gayle of being lovers, which I guess we would have been if one of us had a penis. Can I say the P word on TV? No? Okay. Let's call it the peniynay. Both Gayle and I are prodigious lovers and partakers of the natural, god-given peniynay. I'm sorry but there you have it.

We are not gay because we both need a peniynay, we both love the peniynay; but it has to be attached, naturally, at the groin. But we are very good friends. Besides, "all Gayle needs is a man and some cake" and she's living her best life and so am I with Steadman, who, as you know, I have been with for nearly twenty years of bliss.

Donald Trump: I have many good and trusted friends.

Jesus: I am your friend. I will bear all your sins and grieves. Just pray and I will always be your faithful friend. Amen.

When I put it all together my grand conclusion is: Be a good friend and only keep good friends.

Twenty-two
Frenemies

I have many great friends. But it is from my frenenemies that I have learned the most about myself. Looking back I can see through the glass clearly. And at 40, I can honestly say that many times, my enemies have not been the persons I have expected, but, in fact, have been disguised as friends. I think it is a mistake to think your enemies are only those people who openly dislike you. I have come to realize that some of the most dangerous foes can be those closest to you, those who are supposed to "like" you. It is from those types you learn the most about yourself.

Even among friends, I believe there can be competition, envy, and dishonesty. There is no perfect friendship—except maybe for Oprah and Gayle. But even between them, there are probably issues that they both learn and grow from. It is a question of degree. To what degree is someone competitive, envious or dishonest? The question is not whether my friendship with someone is imperfect but whether it is so toxic that it prevents you from growing as individual in the manner you want and need to grow, and instead thwarts you, brings out the worse in me, tears you down.

I have learned this about myself: I abhor competitiveness among friends. I get hurt when someone I consider a friend seems to want to "outdo" me at every juncture. I don't like to feel like I am competing with friends or that they are competing with me. It doesn't feel good. If something happens to my friend and it's good, I want to share in their happiness just like I would want them to reciprocate. If something good happens to me and I tell a friend and I get a response that is less than enthusiastic, I get depressed.

It is natural to be happy and enthusiastic when good things happen to your friends I think. Otherwise, maybe these so called friends are just actors. They are not real friends and if you refuse to heed the warning signs, you're going to get deeply hurt by them somewhere down the road. My feeling is that you should not have to choke a compliment from a friend when a compliment is clearly due. It is natural to shower your friends with compliments and words of encouragement. This is love. This is showing love. Any one who is all criticism (which they will tell you is for your own good) cannot be a true friend. Criticism has its purpose and place; but everybody needs praise from time to time.

I also feel that you should not have to fear telling a friend good news. I have had friends with whom I have felt more camaraderie when I have problems and my life was the pits. I have had friends who seemed to enjoy my company more when I did not have love in my life, when I was man-less, jobless and even penniless. I felt really liked and popular with certain people then, but the minute I got a job, or god forbid, a man, the fangs came out and the fault finding would begin. Some people will like you more when you lack and they have, and if you're not careful they will "advise" you out of having anything good in your life. There are other people I have considered friends who did the opposite. They were around for a good laugh, long conversations about nothing, and outings. But when trouble hit and the weather got a little gray, they would disappear.

Neither one of these types are true friends. To me, they are enemies disguised as friends. But guess what? It's important to love them anyway because at least, they teach you what not to be. It is as important to know what not to be as it is to know what to be. It is important to love any teacher who teaches you any lesson that helps to advance your life to the next level. Oh, Mr. Trump will tell you "if they screw you screw them back." And I'm not going to say that isn't appropriate sometimes. But even he is mellowing and realizing that it is better not to waste precious time on vengeance and getting even.

If I talked to Oprah, Donald Trump and Jesus I think they would say the following:

Oprah: See, I don't get that. I have a lot of friends and I've never had that experience. My best friend Gayle and I are closer than any sister relationship. I can't go a day without talking to Gayle. She wishes the best for me and I do the same for her. I always tell Gayle, "You're the reason I never got married." And Gayle says to me, "you're the reason I got divorced." There is no envy or competition between us. She wants the best for me as I do for her, always.

Donald Trump: Love my frenemies? That's the dumbest thing I ever heard! Dump those losers! Why would I want to waste time with people who took up space and who didn't wish me well and weren't happy for me? Look, I've been around the block a few times and I know that nobody wishes anybody well. "They all want what you have, your wife, your dog, your cat, your business, your TV show. They want your ideas. They want your deals." They even want your eyes and other body parts when you die. Call me paranoid but I don't trust anybody. People like that former governor of New York who shall remain nameless make it very hard for me to trust anybody. Can you imagine this s.o.b. told me that he 'didn't want to bother the

Secretary' when I asked for a perfectly normal favor, after I had supported him by pouring money in his campaign? That's the definition of frenemy right there. I don't advocate loving anybody who double crosses you and who is not happy for you and doesn't help you when you ask for perfectly "acceptable favors." Do not even play golf with those parasites. Cut em loose, blast them in your books, and hang out with guys like Regis. (Unless and until he pisses you off.)

Jesus: Be ye kind one to another, tender hearted, forgiving one another as I your father have forgiven you. If someone hurts you, turn the other cheek. Live in peace with your friends and frenemies. Amen.

When I put it all together, my grand conclusion is: it is possible to have a healthy friendship that does not involve envy and competition; at the same time, sometimes friends are not there for you when you expect them to be. Be big enough to forgive them most of the time; if what they did is egregious however Mr. Trump makes it clear that you can blast them in your books and never talk to them again.

Twenty-Three
Who do you dress for?

Was it Shakespeare who said, "To thine own self be true"?" There has never been a truer admonishment. A lot of people, women in particular, dress for other people. They either dress to please men, or they dress to impress other women. They become fashion slaves, putting things onto their bodies that frankly have no business being on their body. I know I am guilty of many sartorial infractions.

It took me forty long years, but finally, I think I have the wardrobe thing down pat: Wear what makes me happy. It doesn't matter if people think I am not dressing my age. It doesn't matter if they gossip and say among their friends, "who does she think she is?" "Where does she think she's going?"

It's not any body's business what anybody else wears. What does dressing your age even mean? I see some hot looking 40 something year olds out there who are extremely toned, and who can give any twenty-something a run for their money. Look at Nicolette Sheridan and Demi Moore. Look at Halle Berry and Nicole Kidman. Look at Janet Jackson and Tyra Banks. Oh, wait. Tyra is thirty something. But you get my point, right? Forty-something women are smoking hot these days. There is no typical forty year old so I am not sure how forty should look and I am not sure how one would dress one's age.

For me, it's very simple: buy quality not quantity. Edit frequently. Invest in good fabrics and good tailoring. Be sparing with fads and generous with classics that can be worn year after year. Wear dark colors to work like Black, Navy and Brown (especially if you are in a professional job.) Make sure it fits. Show less than more. Don't wear anything overly tight, especially tops because it could inadvertently send the wrong message to the wrong people. (Don't get me wrong. There are times when it is okay to show a little cleavage, or wear a knit top that shows that you have breasts. But for me, I don't want this to be my staple. There's only one Pam Anderson and she wears it well.) Be comfortable in your clothes; that is what dressing your age should be about. Certainly, it is what dressing is about for me.

For entertainment, wear jeans. I love denim and think it was a great invention. It is totally ageless and age-appropriate for anyone, so long as there are no holes in the crotch. Most people probably can pull off the holes-in-the-crotch look. I definitely can't. I would keep trying to cover the hole and that shows I lack confidence and that would totally ruin the look. On formal occasions, I have figured out that the trick is to wear a black dress, a nice black patent leather pump and have a man on your arm (even if he's gay), or don't go cause you'll just look ridiculous.

If I talked to Oprah, Donald Trump and Jesus I think they would say the following:

Oprah: I think its time to do away this notion of "dressing for your age. " I never really knew what that meant. There are all these rules in effect, like don't wear white after Labor Day. Who made these rules? Ladies, I say, wear what makes you happy. Live your best life. Just don't show up on the Oprah show nude. That's where I draw the line.

Donald: I could care less about what I wear and how my wardrobe is perceived. I am more interested in seeing "what a beautiful woman is wearing." I think it does matter a great deal what a woman wears, how she carries herself. I see a lot of young women in Hollywood who are "undressed" in public. When Britney took off her pannies (spelled, PANTIES), well, it was sad. It was Anna Nicole Smith all over again. If my daughter did that I would be embarrassed. I would be very disappointed. Did I mention Ivanka went to Wharton? Whatever you say about Paris Hilton, I think she basically dresses well. She pulls off her attire well or her lack of attire. Britney doesn't pull it off so well. But I wish Britney well. I hope her family can get her some help.

Jesus: Your body is a temple. Your body is the kingdom of God. Present yourself the way you would the temple of God and the Kingdom of God. Amen.

When I put it all together, my grand conclusion is: There are no rules for dressing so long as one wears underwear in public and so long as one respects oneself and one's body and not pull a Britney Spears; that's not a good look if you're over twenty-five.

Twenty-four
Wear comfortable Jimmy Choos (but buy a condo first)

What could possibly be more miserable than uncomfortable, ill-fitting shoes? Shoes that are too high, too tight, too narrow, and too big? This is so ridiculous. Shoes should fit your life. Shoes are a metaphor for your life.

I think of my younger days and I cringe when I think about all the times I wore shoes that were uncomfortable and wrong for me. What was I thinking? All in the name of fashion I would suffer stupidly in some shoe that was too high or too tight or something else that was wrong with it, because I thought the shoes made me look so sexy, or sophisticated or something. How wrong I was. No one can look sexy in shoes that do not fit right, and that are not comfortable. If your feet are not happy, you are not going to be sexy no matter what delusions you may have swimming in your head. The right shoes are fundamental. Besides, when I look at some women in their forties and beyond and I see how disfigured their feet have become from ill fitting shoes, I just cringe. It doesn't have to be like that. You can be sexy and wear the right shoes. I am not saying to get granny shoes that make you look old and thick ankled. But maybe you can forgo the six inch stilettos for walking around the city, or maybe you can wear a size nine instead of the size seven and a half (when your feet are size ten.) There is nothing more unproductive than wasting time being uncomfortable in one's shoes.

Jeeze. I must sound old. No self-respecting fashionista would be caught dead in anything lower than a six inch stiletto. Well, whatever. Kill your feet if you wish. I know I'm not going to do it. I don't care how old it makes me sound.

Speaking of comfortable shoes, I have been itching to buy myself a pair of Jimmy Choo black patent leather pumps (no more than three inches.) This is probably going to cost me close to a thousand dollars by the time I get the money together. Oprah is rumored to have more than 200 pairs of Jimmy Choos. Though, I'm not trying to be her. That would be asinine since Oprah can probably buy the whole Jimmy Choo company. Actually she is so rich she doesn't even have to pay for her Jimmy Choos. People just send them to her by the boat loads for free. I want to know what it feels like to own a pair of Jimmy Choos which I bought with my hard earned money. I want to know what it feels like to own just one pair. It is on my list for this year, to buy myself a pair of Jimmy Choos as a fortieth birthday present to myself. The only thing is I am really conflicted about this because in the *Millionaire Next Door* by Thomas Stanley and William Danko, they specifically disdain this kind of exorbitant purchase. Most millionaires in America, according to them, would never, ever, spend this kind of money on shoes. As a result, they are "prodigious accumulators of wealth" whereas I'm a recovering bankrupt, and an under accumulator of wealth. I don't want to always be an under accumulator of wealth my whole entire life. How can I square their philosophy with my desires and how do I square my desires with what I have learned about spending money you don't have? I want to be responsible. I do not want to be wasteful.

The trick, I think, is to defer my gratification a little bit. I can easily just go to Saks right now and charge it on my credit card but I will not do that. I want to take $1,000 in cash to the store and buy myself this pair of shoe. So you know what I'm going to do? I'm going to do it the Robert Kiyosaki way. In his book, *Guide to Becoming Rich* he espouses a philosophy that I like. He advocates living life to the hilt, having the luxurious life you crave, and getting what you want, but making sure to have an asset with which you can offset a debt. He advocates only having "good debt." He sees luxury as divinity. I agree with Mr. Kiyosaki.

So, in order to get my Jimmy Choo shoe, I am going to find myself a condominium. I am going to buy it for as little down as possible, and I'm going to get a tenant in there to pay me at least one thousand dollars more than the monthly mortgage in rent. The very first rental check I get, I am going to go out and buy myself the black patent leather Jimmy Choo because unlike those frugal Scots in the *Millionaire Next door*, I really want to have my cake and eat it too. I could never be one of them. There's only so much deprivation I can deal with.

If I talked to Oprah, Donald Trump and Jesus I think they would say the following:

Oprah: A friend just sent me over 200 pairs of Jimmy Choos. I've had to build an addition to my shoe closet in my house in California just to store these Choos....actually it may have been my house in Hawaii...or was it the one in Chicago? I don't remember. I have to ask Gayle. But I am going to keep all the Choos and give them to my girls in South Africa for their 18th birthdays. For myself, I prefer Christian Louboutin. That's my shoe du jour. I've just stocked up on

99 pairs. Ninety-nine pairs help me Jesus! That's what I call living my best life!

Donald: I've discovered that true comfort in shoes is directly correlated to the price of the shoe.

Jesus: I wore sandals when I walked in Jerusalem. I say go barefoot rather than spoil your feet with ill-fitting shoes. That is the will of your father. Amen.

When I put it all together my grand conclusion is: Unless you have multiple houses like Oprah, you don't need 200 pairs of shoes. But you can indulge yourself so long as you take care of the important things first—like getting rental real estate.

Twenty five
Mud baths

A good mud bath can be good for the skin but too much mud can block your nasal passages and next thing you know you can't breathe. I can't help but remember when Donald Trump and Barbara Walters had the falling out over Rosie O'Donnell. Meredith Vieira got in on the action and asked Trump during an interview on the Today Show, "Why would you want to get into all that mudslinging." Mr. Trump nearly tore up Meredith. I was actually scared for Meredith as I sat on the edge of my seat watching. I was thankful when Ivanka jumped in and stopped her father from the massacre he was about to perpetrate on the talk show host. I couldn't believe how close Meredith allowed herself to get to being a carcass.

I sure am not going to render an opinion about this epic fight between these heavy hitters because they will squash me like a bug. All I'm going to say is it's probably not a good idea to sling mud at Barbara. Do not, as Star Jones said, "denigrate Ms. Walters." You will not win. This is a good rule. And I am learning that it is not just Ms. Walters we should be careful not to denigrate, it's anybody. Denigrating others and slinging mud only creates bad blood and burns bridges. It is true what they say about burning bridges. I should know. I have burned many a bridge in my day. And I am sure I will burn a few more before the curtains come down. But the important thing is not the number of bridges I have burned, but the number of bridges I could have burned but didn't. Those are the times in life when you grow as a person, the moments when you take the high road even though a lower road would be so much easier to take.

It is not easy to do this a lot of times. Because there are unfortunately many people who only understand one language: MUD. If you don't throw mud at them and hit them in the face with it, they think you are weak and a push over and they try to take advantage of you and to injure you and cause you pain. So there are times when you not only have to sling the mud, you have to burn the bridge and you have to denigrate and you have to make an example of an individual so that "others can see what you are capable of, and think twice before messing with you." But I think that where at all possible, avoid mud. Donald and Barbara are rich and I'm sure they will kiss and make up eventually. But for the average person, mudslinging can really destroy perfectly good relationships which no amount of money can buy back.

If I talked to Oprah, Donald Trump and Jesus I think they would say the following:

Oprah: I love bubble baths but I just don't do mud baths. I don't like 'em. I don't do 'em. They get in the way of living my best life. When people say bad things about me, or try to get me into public squabbles, I just ignore them, as if they don't exist. I am sure it infuriates them and frustrates them. Nobody wants to be ignored, especially bullies slinging mud. But I ignore 'em.

Donald Trump: If they sling mud at you, throw it back into their faces and let them choke on it. Do not allow anybody to mess with you, especially publicly and get away with it. Make an example of them so that everybody else thinks twice before they throw mud at you. And understand that the truth is the truth. Saying the truth is not the same as throwing mud. For example, if someone is fat they are fat. If they throw mud at you and you call them fat in response, this is fair game. A woman who is fat and throws mud at me probably would not be invited onto the Miss Universe Pageant. Great beauty usually comes with thinness, and other features. But generally speaking thinness is a prerequisite to great beauty; but there are exceptions. And for once, I did not make that rule. I am not trying to be obnoxious. I am not trying to be politically incorrect. The rules were made by society. Thinness in women is usually valued more than fatness in society, but, again, there are exceptions. A man does not have to be beautiful but he should have ample income. He should be able to buy a building that costs USD $1 million dollars without too much trouble. This has nothing to do with Donald Trump so don't throw mud at Donald Trump for saying what everybody thinks and believes, namely, a man can be fat but not broke; a fat woman is hardly ever attractive, with a few exceptions. Look at Star Jones. She is a friend of mine. I have never seen her look more beautiful since she lost the weight. She looks so good she turned off her audience on the View. If someone is not beautiful they are not beautiful. If you call them ugly, it is not mud. If someone is short and you say, "hey shorty," it is not mud. I have said that I was surprised by George Clooney's height. Understand the difference between truth and mud. There is a big difference between truth and mud.

Jesus: Do not fling mud lest it hit an angel. Amen.

When I put it all together, my grand conclusion is: Be nice. Don't say bad things about people. If they say bad things about you and it potentially damages your reputation, call them on it, even if you have to do it publicly. If it is possible to ignore bullies who try to sully your name or reputation without cause, ignore them. If you can't, let them have it. But the rule "if you can't say something nice don't say anything," is a good rule.

Life is just a Rubrics Cube

Twenty-six
A good doc is hard to find

Even if you never had a real doctor, you'll turn 40, and you'll realize that at the bare minimum, you may need to get yourself a reproductive endocrinologist (if you're female). Why? Well, time is running out and if a man fails drop from Heaven in your lap pretty soon and sperminate you pretty quick, you may need to buy the sperm. That means that sperm will start arriving at your apartment in tanks and you'll need an endocrinologist to monitor your rendezvous with the turkey baster.

Seriously, it is wise to have a regular doctor and if you're female, a GYN. If you're male, you should have a specialist who can check your prostate when you get to the grand old age of forty. By the way, what is the opposite of GYN? I can't remember. All I know, this is the age where if we're not careful and conscious and paying attention, things tend to start going south. It could be your blood pressure starts to slowly rise, or weird cells begin to grow in places they shouldn't, or you start to accumulate too much cholesterol around the arteries, or whatever. This is also the age where we want to exercise a whole lot less. In my youth, I was a gym rat. If I may say so myself, I was in such good shape, that once some guy stopped driving on the Brooklyn Bridge and backed up all the traffic. I swear I was horrified and flattered all at the same time. I smiled in spite of myself. It was like, idiot, you are backing up the traffic! But he did make me smile. These days, nobody looks at me. And getting to the gym takes a lot of work, scheduling and mind power. Sometimes I wish I could afford a personal trainer to physically haul me there on his shoulders and then put me on a machine that actually does the crunches for me. I would much rather sit at my computer and surf the net, or read, or sleep than go pump iron in some smelly gym. I don't know why it happens, but it happens and so all the more reason to have a regular doctor so that they can remind us during our annual check ups what can happen to a body that doesn't get enough exercise.

Plus, you just want to be able to nip things in the bud, or have somebody to sue for things which should have been nipped in the bud but were not. (Only kidding.) I remember hearing or reading somewhere that Donald Trump does not like doctors. I so get why he doesn't. But not all doctors are scoundrels. Just like not all lawyers are scoundrels. But an unscrupulous doctor is more dangerous than an unscrupulous lawyer. I think. And dentists too. I swear I knew a dentist who saw dollar signs in my mouth. I don't want to think about what some doctors see when they examine their patients. What I don't like is feeling like some doctors see me as either a guinea pig, or as an idiot who can't comprehend anything so they take over my body as if it's not mine and proceed to do whatever they want with it. "Oh no, you don't," I have wanted to say on occasion. But I've started to realize that medicine really is a service industry. If I am not getting the service I need, rather than hate or distrust all doctors, find a new one. Still, I am getting to the point where I don't want to have to keep up this never ending search for this ideal practitioner anymore. I just want to find a good generalist, a good specialist (GYN), and a good endocrinologist (just in case I need him.) and I'll be good to go.

If I talked to Oprah, Donald Trump and Jesus I think they would say the following:

Oprah: I love doctors. They are my friends. They keep me living my best life!

Donald Trump: I hate doctors. Next to lawyers they are the biggest crooks.

Jesus: Lawyers, tax collectors, doctors....pray to the Lord thy God. He will heal you and save you from evil doers. But remember that not all who say lord, lord, is righteous. Do not judge, lest ye be judged. Amen

When I put it all together, my grand conclusion is: Better just to stay healthy if at all possible so as to avoid the headache of fixing your broken health—that is potentially perilous.

Twenty-seven
Good health is worth three billion dollars

If the life genie gave me a choice between good health and having three billion dollars like Donald Trump, I would ask for both. But if I could only have one, it would be a no brainer. I would choose the three billion dollars. No, I'm only kidding. I value my health above all things. I would rather stay in financial dire straits and have my health, than have three billion dollars and be sick. And obviously I am talking about having more than just the common cold. I am talking about terminal sickness. The good thing is, I've never heard of really rich people who had to choose between their wealth and their health. In fact, people who are financially abundant are usually in abundantly good health too. Abundance seems to beget abundance.

Good health cannot be underrated. And if the author of *The Big 40* is right, most 40 year olds value their health and describe themselves as being in good health, and this is fabulous.

Like most people, I really appreciate my health. I do not take that for granted. I see too much out there, I know how quickly things can change. We are all so fragile. It's not as if I didn't understand the value of good health all along. It's just that I have grown to really appreciate my health; I have grown to respect my health. I have grown to understand that is it up to me to maintain good physical, emotional, mental and spiritual health. Like everything else, good health takes work. It takes focus. It takes sacrifice.

I guess it's true that the best things in life are free. And if you think about it, good health is actually free. It is a question of "free" will. We are all free to eat, drink and be merry. We are free to exercise or be a coach potato. We are free to engage in high risk illicit sex. We are free to be Vegan. We are free to eat meat. We are free to always use a condom. We are free to associate with people who live wholesomely and in communion with nature. We are free to take drugs; we are free to eat at McDonalds every day and to be addicted to MacDonald's fries. We are free to cook with trans fats or olive oil. We are free to only eat organic foods. We are free to jog, run, and play basketball. We are free to take daily walks. We are free to avoid stressful situations. We are free to only eat when we are hungry and to stop eating when we are full. We are free to do 100 sit-ups every day. We are free to think good thoughts. We are free to avoid sugar. We are free to avoid fats. We are free to smoke or not to smoke.

You see? It is cause and effect. Good health is really a matter of free will, it's a question of freedom and whether we will respect or abuse our freedom of choices.

What I "know for sure" (in addition to the fact that I am not Oprah) is prevention is key. The choices we made in the past and continue to make today will decide the quality of our health in the future. No one can expect to be strong and robust when they are old, if they abuse their bodies when they are young. It is when we are young that we should be strengthening our bodies for old age. One cannot reasonably expect to abuse one's body in youth by not exercising, overeating, taking drugs, eating too much sugar, drinking excessively, smoking, being a couch potato, injecting steroids, continuously placing oneself in stressful situations, engaging in high risk illicit sex, not investing in one's health, not planning for one's older years, and still have a strong, healthy body when one gets old. "Looking good for one's age" is a life-time investment. Plastic surgery can only help so much. After a while, you get so stretched out, your eyes take on a weird countenance.

Knowing this, I am making the choice to be strong and healthy. That is going to mean making sacrifices. I am free to make these choices. And I am so glad to be forty because it really sinks in finally, that even in health, it is up to me. It's about the way I think and the way I act.

If I talked to Oprah, Donald Trump and Jesus I think they would say the following:

Oprah: If you are living your best life, it means you are also taking care of your health. You shouldn't have to choose between good health and money. I know there are many people in this country who can't afford healthcare. So money does have an impact the state of a person's health. But there are many things you can do, to prevent illnesses even with little or no money. For example, don't smoke. Don't do drugs. You will read that I have used drugs in my youth.

That is why I am an advocate of no drugs because I know it is not good for you. Eat a vegetable everyday.

Donald: I have not been sick in nearly fifteen years. A part of that has to do with the fact that I don't shake people's hands. People are full of germs. Nobody should shake hands with anybody. It is such an unhealthy thing to do. I think people should bow when they greet each other, like they do in some Asian countries. I do not usually get sick. I think there is some correlation between health and wealth. Most of my friends hardly ever get sick. And most of my friends are rich. Sickness is often an affliction of the poor. I say, get rid of poverty, get rid of sickness. That's why you should read my book, *Think Big and Kick Ass*. That book will help you to stop getting sick because it gives you the tools to get rich.

Jesus: When I lived in Galilee, Nazareth, Jerusalem and Bethlehem, there were many sick people whom I healed. If you believe in me you too can be healed; and you can heal the sick. Amen.

When I put it all together, my grand conclusion is: In your prayers it is important to ask not only for financial abundance, but abundantly good health too—which is more important than all the money in the world.

Twenty-eight
Quit a job that gives you angst (but don't go bankrupt)

Ten years ago, after about two weeks on a job I knew was never going to work out, I got up, took my pocket book, walked out the door of this Park Avenue law firm, pushed the elevator button, got on the elevator, walked to the subway, and rode the F train home. I didn't say a word to anybody. I think they thought I was going to the powder room when I calmly got up and left with my pocket book.

As I walked from the subway to my apartment that morning, I knew I had done something from which there was no going back. I was terrified because I had no money and the rent was due. I had acted impulsively, crazily. But there it was. I quit. People just go to pieces when I tell them this story. They think it's absolutely hysterical that I just walked off my job like that. It wasn't very funny at the time. And the consequences of my actions were dire. I know exactly what Donald Trump would think about this. Look how he chewed out that Apprentice participant when she told him she was quitting? But would Donald Trump stay with a job he hated?

I had my reasons for my actions, let's just leave it at that. But it was both brave and foolhardy what I did because I did not have another job lined up. Boy did I *suffer*. It turns out that that job was the only offer I ever got. In 1998 when I got out of law school the market was not that great for lawyers. Two years after my bold attack of ego, and an exhaustive job hunt, (and the fact that I had failed to handle my money properly before and during law school) I was forced to file bankruptcy. Karma? Maybe. I had to quit the legal profession for several years and I got a job teaching in the inner city schools of Brooklyn in order to put food on the table and pay the rent. Believe me that was another drama, the details of which will fill another book.

I'm here to tell you that sometimes, *a* job is better than no job. But if you are like me, I also say, if a job is giving you angst, take your bags and find another job.

I would not recommend doing it the way I did. It was crazy. I admit it. It was not the appropriate way to leave one's employment and it potentially burns bridges. But more importantly, don't quit a job if you don't have another one lined up. I should have lined up another job then I should have been woman enough to walk into that lawyer's office and tell him that I was quitting because the job was "not what I signed up for." Still, in retrospect, it was meant to be the way it happened. I did the right thing for me at that moment in my journey called life. I learned a lot from it.

I've come a long way since then. Seven years later, by a stroke of total irony, and I swear to god this is the truth, I started my law career, on my own terms, by renting an office on Park Avenue, up the block (literally 2 blocks!) away from that office. It was totally not planned, it just so happened that it was the first office (a cubby hole really) I found after I finally saved up enough money to start my practice. Can you believe it? As Oprah would say, it was a full circle moment. I felt like Cinderella coming to the Ball.

If I talked to Oprah, Donald Trump and Jesus I think they would say the following:

Oprah: Live your best life! Own yourself! There's nothing like it!

Donald: Never be a quitter. Only schmucks quit. But I personally could never have a job where I work for someone else and I hated the job. True, I worked for my father. I learned a lot from him. But he was my father. He was my mentor. I could never work for someone else other than my father. I do have partners on various projects. I am involved with different joint ventures. I am basically a real estate guy. But I have all these other projects involving meats and vodkas and other stuff like water, ties and cuff links. Primarily, I build buildings. My buildings are the best in the world. I don't have to brag. This is a known fact. If a condo is not selling in one of my buildings, I just raise the price. Then it sells like hot cakes. When I shook hands with Mark for the Apprentice, I liked him right away. I knew I could trust him. We decided to go fifty fifty. That Apprentice who quit was a loser. I was in shock that she would quit just because she didn't like it. Never do that. That's just schmuckish. But, would I work for someone else in a job I hated? Are you crazy? I guess technically when I do the TV show for NBC Jeff Zucker is my boss in the sense that he pays me a hefty signing fee. Believe me a lot of negotiation went into it. But if you really think about it, they are working for me. They promote my show. I told them, look, "I know what you paid Jennifer Anniston on Friends." They call me on my birthday at five in the morning and wish me happy birthday before my own wife does. But to say I would ever have a Nine to Five Job for somebody else and stay with it even though I hated it? Never. I employ a lot of people in my various enterprises, including my casinos, hotels, golf courses. I work building buildings. "I do it to do it." I don't need money. I do what I love. I could never work doing something I don't love. But you should never quit. Quitting is bad news. Quitting is for schmucks.

Jesus: Let not your heart be troubled. When you are feeling angst from a job you hate, remember that your Father in heaven wants the best for you. He is your Shepherd who will anoint your head with oil and prepare a table for you in the presence of your enemies. You want another job? Ask, and it shall be given. Seek and ye shall find. Knock and another job's door shall open to you. Amen.

When I put it all together, my grand conclusion is: Everything has a price. If you can't pay the price, think twice before getting the merchandise. But don't suffer on a job. Too much of our lives are spent at work. One should be happy at work.

Twenty-nine
Make up your mind!

People say I'm capricious and I say, what else to you expect from a Capricorn? I do change my mind a lot and it can be infuriating, especially to people who write in their appointment book with a pen. I always tell people, pencil me in do not ink me in because I could change my mind. Why should I have to feel bad about changing my mind? Isn't that a woman's prerogative? At forty, I've never been more woman than I am now, so it seems to me that I have an even greater right to change my mind if I feel the need.

Okay. I admit that taken to the extreme, this can be a very selfish and inconsiderate thing to be. To some extent, people have to be able to depend on your word. If you say you are going skiing in Vermont with your friends, and this has been the plan for two months, and everybody has written it down in pen, it's not okay, absent a real emergency like horrific menstrual cramps or busted plumbing, to back out on the day itself. That is just rude and inconsiderate. But there are other times that a woman should be able to change her mind without getting dirty looks. For one thing, a woman should be able to change her mind about which candidate she will vote for president. A woman should be able to change her mind about allowing her date to get to second base on the twelfth date. A woman should be able to change her mind about buying a pair of Jimmy Choos before she buys a condominium.

    I guess the problem with capriciousness is when it keeps you from achieving and from moving forward in your life. People who are capricious tend to move backwards and in many different directions. They can't make up their minds. They get analysis paralysis. The miss opportunities because they are always busy doing that internal debate: should I? Shouldn't I? They make the same decision a thousand times; then change their minds. This is very bad. This is not cute. This is a big problem. If all that was at stake was a pair of Jimmy Choos it would be one thing. But when your whole life is hanging in the balance, it is quite another thing. Rather than being so famous for "changing your mind," it might be better to be famous for being able to make up your mind; but give yourself the option to change it if *absolutely* necessary.

If I talked to Oprah, Donald Trump and Jesus I think they would say the following:

Oprah: It is a woman's prerogative to change her mind. Live your best life!

Donald Trump: It's a woman's prerogative that is why you must always get a prenup.

Jesus: The Lord thy God changes his mind all the time and turns back his wrath from those upon whom he could justifiably unleash his wrath. Be merciful to others as he is merciful to you. amen.

When I put it all together my grand conclusion is: It is a woman's prerogative to change her mind, but it may not be in her best interest to be so capricious all the time.

Thirty
Ask, but don't nag

One of the most influential books I have read recently *The Secret*, by Rhonda Byrne is a great book to read if, like me, you consider yourself a late bloomer, and you are not sure how to turn things around. (Oprah apparently loves the book; I just read that on Wikipedia, so that gives it more credibility right there!) I totally agree with a lot of the things Byrne writes and advocates in this book. And not just because Oprah likes it. Byrne talks about the laws of attraction, she talks about the power of thoughts, she talks about the "magic and magnificence" of nature, and of the universe, and that we, all of us, can have the life we want if we believe in our own power to create that life. She says the first step to getting what we want is to ask for it. This is very powerful stuff. I believe in this stuff.

But there is one thing she says that I disagree with. She says that we only have to *ask once* and that we should never ask over and over again. She could be right. But I don't necessarily agree that this is true all the time. First of all, I say to myself, how does she know that we only have to ask once? Did the universe tell her so? Or is this just her feeling?

When I think back, way back to my childhood, I realize that there were times I asked just once and got stuff, but there were many times (most of the time) when I literally had to nag my mother in order to be heard so that I could get what I want. Case in point, I wanted a cabbage patch doll and had to keep repeating that desire over and over till my mother was convinced that I wasn't too old to have one. I had to nag my mother about getting many an outfits over the course of my childhood and adolescence. In most situations, I have had to ask and persist in order to get the smallest crumb.

When you were a kid didn't your mom sometimes give you what you asked for simply to shut you up, and get you out of her face? Not that I'm suggesting that this is always a good thing. You don't want to annoy the universe. You want to get what you ask for and you want it to be good for you. If you are annoying, and you over-ask, you may get what you asked for but it may not be good for you, because you got it by aggravating somebody and so it is marked with bad energy.

So you have to be reasonable, conscientious and careful. Do not annoy the universe. Don't ask every minute for the same exact thing. Wait a little bit. See what transpires. But by all means, don't ask just once if you feel that a little nudging is in order. If you are scared to go against what Rhonda says, preface your requests by saying, "I know I run the risk of annoying you, but this is not the intention. I only ask again to remind you that I am waiting patiently for you to grant my wish...." I think if you are polite about it, and if you use a little humor with it, and if you offer something in return (make a deal!) that you just might get what you want a little faster.

The thing is it, I really feel that in asking God, or the universe for something, one has to be mindful that God is a very busy guy and sometimes he doesn't give us something right away because it just straight up slips his mind--that's why he needs to be reminded from time to time. Sure he probably has clerical help, but it's still a lot he has to do. No, I'm serious. God has a lot to do up there with creating new galaxies to keep man spinning his wheels, to figuring out what to do with the problems in Africa, to figuring out whether to rid New York of Raid resistant cockroaches, to deciding whether he's going to stop Hurricane Susan from decimating South America, or whether he'll just let it run its course.

Plus, he has all those babies to deliver and has to decide who's going to be what and where he's going to put them. And I'm sure he gets a lot of calls from politicians. Believe me there's a lot of people and issues that God has to deal with. So if you are the quiet type who goes and sits in a corner and only asks once, you run the risk that you will get tended to last, if at all, and not out of malice or anything. Just simply because you were not assertive enough, or you were too nice and God figured you wouldn't mind waiting. Next thing you know, you're forty and you're still waiting!

Sometimes you have to make noise. Sometimes you have to ask a second and third time. Sometimes you have to tap God on the shoulder, or pull his little toe and say, "Father, I am still waiting!" And don't be afraid to make a deal. Say, you know what God, if you do this for me, here's what I'll do for you. But only promise what you can deliver. God doesn't have the greatest sense of humor, I've come to realize. And I say that with all due respect. Don't play around with God. He's a very serious man.

The test is one of reasonableness, I think. It is nice only to ask once and to sit and be patient. But nice can sometimes leave you holding the bag. When you get to be forty or older, and you realize that time is not necessarily on your side, so you better get better at asking--even if that means more than once. Just be sure that what you are asking for is really what you need and want because woe will be yours if it's not.

If I talked to Oprah, Donald Trump and Jesus I think they would say the following:

Oprah: If you feel you need to ask more than once in order to get what you want so that you can live your best life, then, by all means, ask more than once. Ask for what you need.

Donald: Patience is a virtue. I have waited decades to get what I wanted in some instances. I am a very patient man. Sometimes it's a lack of patience that makes you seem like a nag. Do not nag. It just makes a nuisance of you and nobody likes a nuisance. I would never hire a nuisance. I would never marry a nag. I doubt that God likes a nag or would give a nag diddle squat. So be careful. "It could be trouble."

Jesus: Ask and ye shall receive. Amen.

When I put it all together, my grand conclusion is: Don't nag. But ask the life genie for what you want and you will receive it. Just make sure you really want it.

Thirty-one
Even rich people have problems (behold Jennifer Anniston)

By the time you get to be forty, you come to realize you are always going to have problems, no matter what, so you might as well get used to it and develop problem solving skills. Because if you don't you will end up with all kinds of stress related illnesses like ulcers and diabetes and your face will sag so bad you'll look like Blanche (from the Golden Girls) looking down on that mirror.

Even the very rich have problems. The trick, I am learning, is to stay on top of your problems, to always be a little bigger than the biggest problem you face. How does one do that? Well, everybody has to develop their own strategies and techniques. I can tell you that since I read the book, *Secrets of a Millionaire Mind,* by T Harv Eker, I've become obsessed with staying or growing bigger than my problems. And for the most part, I do it by just repeating to myself: "I am bigger than any problem I face." I get into this meditative state and it's amazing how well it works to keep me confident and to push me through the walls, up to the higher level of awareness and accomplishment.

Now, it is totally true that I have not been challenged in a way that some people have been challenged. Look at Jennifer Anniston. That was a big problem having such a public break up and watching your husband take up with a pillow-lipped, big breasted, heroin chic Hollywood icon turned United Nations Ambassador and philanthropist who has a penchant for adopting exotic babies--and leaving you with all your gorgeous hair. I always searched Jen's face for cracks, but there was nothing, only elegance, poise and a stiff upper lip. I greatly admired her for that. She must have suffered so much, but it never showed publicly. She grew herself to be bigger than all that public scrutiny and ridicule, and she did it quickly, in a matter of days, and when she did speak of Brad, it was only with praise.

Don't get me wrong. Angelina and Brad are cool. They do a lot of good for society. Their family is gorgeous. And you know Brad is going to run for President in 2016 and he's going to win and Angelina will be America's first lady. But I admire Jen's stoicism and her grace and I know she is going to find the most wonderful guy who will never leave her one of these days.

And I am not going to sit here and be a hypocrite and pretend I could have been so big and strong like Jennifer. I would have likely fallen apart. I would have broken down and cried in public. I would have called my ex-husband names on Larry King Live and then I would have gone and ripped out all of Angelina's hair and spun her skinny ass round and round and that would have created havoc because Angelina Tomb Raider can totally kick *my* ass. So, there is a lot of room for me to grow to be even bigger than I am.

There are people with even bigger more complex problems than Jennifer, I am sure. Oprah has problems. It must have been a big problem when those Texas beef ranchers sued her in Amarillo, Texas, over her comments on beef. I remember seeing her egress from her private jet in Amarillo with her puppies in tow, and I remember thinking, oh my god, she looks like she feels weak in the knees! Well, she overcame that and won the suit; and she was unapologetic for something she shouldn't have to apologize for. She was even defiant when she said: "I still don't like beef" after the case was over. I admired her strength in the face of big problems. Now, there are other problems. It must have been a big problem when her school in South Africa came under scrutiny for child abuse. It is going to be a very big problem if Obama wins the Democratic nomination in 2008 and loses the national election. I wouldn't want to be Oprah then.

Did Jesus have problems? Yes, big ones. The guy got crucified.

Donald Trump has problems too it's just that his are billion dollar problems that come with billion dollar headaches. He said in his book, *Think Big and Kick Ass,* "my business is so hard sometimes I feel like Sisyphus who was condemned to roll a boulder uphill for eternity." When I read that, I thought, damn. What problem have I had on that scale? None, and I don't want any either. Mine are big enough, thank you.

I have noticed that life seldom gives you the same exact problem twice. It may give you a similar problem, to see if you remember the answer (because life is just a test) but it is not going to give you the exact same fact pattern because the universe knows that the first time, it's a problem. The second time, you're like, are you freaking kidding me? The trick, while you're getting roasted, is to remember to grow yourself to be bigger than the problem, and to know you're not going to get roasted on the barbecue grill forever.

If I talked to Oprah, Donald Trump and Jesus I think they would say the following:

Oprah: If problems are bogging you down, you can't live your best life. I think the idea of making yourself bigger than the problems is smart. Be smart. I was always smart. I never thought of myself as the prettiest girl in the room, even though I have won beauty pageants; but I was one of the smartest. Smart girls make themselves bigger than their problems. They do not allow life and problems to get the better of them. They stand up and face the problems head on, even if they are a little scared.

Donald: I am the greatest problem solver in the United States, possibly the world. That is why I am a billionaire. I handle pressure, I solve problems. That's why I get paid. That's my job: solve problems. No problem is too big for me to fix. The bigger the problem, the more motivated I get to solve it, the more fun I have. Not everybody has this talent for solving problems. If you've got, you've got it. If you don't have it, you can't develop it, except in rare circumstances. Winners are born. I am starting to think success is innate. It's usually the same people who enjoy it; it's usually the same people who lose all the time. Watch out for people who can't deal with their problems. They are usually not winners. Think twice about shaking hands with people who are not winners. Do you want that to rub off on you? Try to hang around winners exclusively. Stay far away from people who can't handle problems and pressure.

Jesus: Prayer changes everything. Losers can become winners with prayer. Prayers can solve problems. Amen.

When I put it all together my grand conclusion is: Don't get bogged down by problems because it gets in the way of living your best life. The more problems you can solve, the more valuable you will be to yourself and others. When the going gets tough, a little prayer can't hurt.

Thirty-two
Life is just a rubrics cube

By forty, you start to rethink everything. You start to wonder what it's all really about. You start to ask some real tough questions. My grand forty year old conclusion is that life is just a rubrics cube. If you don't take charge of that rubrics cube and get all your colors lined up the way they are supposed to be, confusion will permeate your life. So you can't get anything done. When you are confused, you are not properly grounded, you are rooted in rocky ground, or you are in soil that is not firm. It is very easy for everything and anything to uproot you in that case. It won't even take such a strong wind.

When we get to be this age, most of us come to realize that we are being played in one way or another. Either we are being played by a lover, employer, child, parent, friend, neighbor, advertiser, or worse, ourselves. There is no greater mind play than the one we play with ourselves. We are the ones with the rubrics cube in hand, creating havoc in our own lives. In fact, we are so skilled at "playing" ourselves, that may I suggest that we actually create all those problems we say we have, just so we can have masochistic fun, solving them? This is a totally subconscious game, by the way. Most of us are not even aware of the games we are playing with ourselves. We are not aware that it is we who create one hundred percent of the problems we have by either doing, or refraining from doing something.

We need to get our heads re-screwed. Either we learn to master the rubrics cube, or stop playing with it. We don't have infinite good years left to continue with these ridiculous head games.

If I talked to Oprah, Donald Trump and Jesus I think they would say the following:

Oprah: Get it together! You can't live your best life till you have it together. Get that rubrics cube color coordinated. Do it today!

Donald: People who can't master the rubrics cube in their heads will get mastered by other people.

Jesus: Plant the seeds of your mind in good, strong soil. Pray for strength and courage so that your seeds are rooted in good soil and bear good fruits. . Amen.

When I put them all together my grand conclusion is: Root yourself in good soil in order to get good fruits..

Thirty-three
Pessimism as a motivator

It's not necessarily bad to be a little bit pessimistic when you find that you are not where you could or should be in your life by the time you hit forty. I think it's bad to be outright negative and gloom and doom and not recognize that one is blessed just to be breathing. But I think that a little bit of pessimism is not only human and honest it is useful; especially for late bloomers like me. Seeing the glass half empty is a wake up call to get my act together, because time waits for no one and is passing by while I am busy mellowing and deluding myself with my "half full" rose colored glass. Thinking the glass is half full almost lulls you into a state of complacency, and the next thing you know, you accept less than the maximum that is possible for you; and you'll end up with a lot of wasted time and opportunities that can never be recalled because when you accept less than what is possible, you become unmotivated and lazy and run the risk of stagnating.

Just think, if Edison didn't want more, if he didn't realize that things were not as good as they could be, that more was possible, that the glass was "half empty", we would all still be in darkness because he would have been satisfied with less light possibilities. He would have been satisfied with candles. He would say, "at least I can see. That's good enough for me." If Martin Luther King didn't want more, if he didn't realize that things could be better, if he got complacent and said, "well at least we are not slaves; that's good enough for me," then Blacks would probably still be forced to sit in the back of the bus. If Alexander Graham bell didn't want more, if he didn't see that his glass was half empty--and was totally dissatisfied with that--nobody would have a cell phone today. And let's not talk about Bill Gates' contributions. I bet you that all these people were pessimistic about their circumstances as they were, they were not satisfied with the status quo, even though they were probably optimistic about what their circumstances could be, about their ability to change their circumstances.

If seeing the glass half empty is pessimistic, then pessimism can be a real motivator, I have learned. It is not okay to be content with just breathing, if you are someone who wants more. Just by the mere wanting, makes more possible. Wanting more is not a bad thing. Wanting a full glass is divine, actually. Look at the universe. You will see works of someone who wanted the glass full, who was not content with a glass "half full." He probably sat back and said one day, "hey, wait a minute, this could be so much fuller. This is half empty. I want more. More is possible." And next thing you know, BANG!

At this stage in my life, I realize unequivocally that I can't just sit back and think that life is going to happen to me. I mean, it will happen, but more than likely, when I am not doing the steering, when I am not turning on taps for myself so that I can fill up my glass, I am not going to be getting exactly how much water I need or want or deserve. This means I'm going to continue to be frustrated, thirsty, lacking, behind. Call me a pessimist, I don't care. But it's not okay that my glass is only "half full." That means that it is also "half empty." I want more. I want the maximum. I want a full glass. I deserve it.

If I talked to Oprah, Donald Trump and Jesus I think they would say the following:

Oprah: A glass that is half full is not your best life. If you know it is half empty, take action to fill it up.

Donald: My glass if full to overflowing and I am still not satisfied. I do not understand how anyone can become complacent about a half full glass. This produces a lot of stress for me, actually--the idea that my glass is only half full. I want an infinite number of full glasses. That to me is fun.

Jesus: The alpha and omega are not "half." Be like God. Amen.

When I put it all together, my grand conclusion is: God doesn't know what a half full glass is and no one should be satisfied with a half full glass if it is possible to have a full glass.

Thirty four
Let them see you cry

The notion that after certain age you can't cry anymore is totally preposterous. I can tell you that I probably cry more now, at forty, than I did when I was younger. I cried a lot when I wrote portions of this book. It may be that my hormones are out of whack. I don't know. But I do know that I am utterly incapable of keeping a stiff upper lip and it is for that reason I would never run for political office. When Hilary Clinton tore up before the New Hampshire primary in 2008, I, the world's biggest bawler, was horrified. I was uncomfortable seeing the first serious female contender for the presidency of the United States getting emotional like that. I thought, oh my God, they will never let her live this down. Nobody wants a president who is female *and* feminine too. The country is just not ready for this much estrogen. They are going to think she is weak and the will either vote for Obama or force Bloomberg to enter the race.

  I used to think allowing others to see you cry is to be weak and to make a spectacle of yourself. Someone who could remain stoic in the face of the most difficult emotional situation was a superior being in my book--especially celebrities and other recognizable figures who never crack a tear even when their lives fell apart. Those who fell short were judged harshly. For instance, I thought Omarosa was good TV during the first Apprentice and I enjoyed watching her, but I felt that when she broke down and cried when she got fired in the boardroom, that she totally lost face. She had played the game as the "strong Black woman," and now here she was bawling like a little girl. When Paris Hilton broke down and cried when the cops came to cart her off to prison to do more time, I thought she lost face. Yet, I was bawling because I happen to like Paris. I kept whispering, "Don't let them see you cry Paris!" When Halle Berry cried when she accepted the Oscar, I wished, unreasonably that she had kept her lip stiff instead and given a more toned down, self-controlled soliloquy. That I cried while watching her was beside the point. Yes, I am a total hypocrite on this issue.

I was wrong about Hillary, by the way. She won the New Hampshire primary convincingly and many people claimed that it was her tears that made the difference in the final analysis. So, upon reflection, I decided, you know what? It's okay for a female candidate for the presidency to cry. How many times have I seen Bill Clinton tear up? How many times have I seen other men tear up? It never once entered my mind that they couldn't lead because they have real human emotions. There is nothing wrong, whatsoever, with having human emotions, and showing that to others on occasion. But it definitely cannot be something that happens all the time. It has to be done discriminately and judiciously.

We are in this thing together, called life. It is quite a journey marked with pain, sorrow, loss and suffering. None of us gets out alive. None of us gets out unscathed. Why is it that we put so much emphasis on the stiff upper lip when an occasion clearly calls for tears? I think it may have come from the British, this sense that showing emotions is bad. The stoic British. It is they who talk about the stiff upper lip of their royals and other citizens. They really give great value to those who can hide their emotions. But it may not necessarily be a good thing to pretend to be a robot when you're not. That was the message I got from Princess Diana.

As I said, it is completely hypocritical of me to expect other people to keep a stiff upper lip when I am so emotional and my lips are so destructible. I cry at the drop of a hat. Last week, I burst into tears at court because I thought the Court was being totally inhuman to my client in a bitter custody case. The Law Guardian took one look at me and barked, "Cut that out! You're a lawyer!" I was *so* embarrassed.

If I talked to Oprah, Donald Trump and Jesus I think they would say the following:

Oprah: Everybody knows how easily I cry. I do it all the time on my show. There's nothing wrong with showing emotions. We are all emotional creatures. I think if tears are appropriate, let them fall. Live your best life.

Donald Trump: I am not big on a man crying. I am a traditional guy. If I ever cry, I would never disclose it and I certainly would not do it in public. That's just not going to happen. I can't have people seeing me go to pieces and fall apart, it would destroy my credibility. It would destroy my business. People would just lose their respect. My cachet would be gone. No. Tears are appropriate in private; except girls and old ladies who can cry without rebuke. A real man should not cry in public. And when Hillary Clinton tore up in New Hampshire? I don't know. I don't have any comment about that.

Jesus: Save your tears for the day when the Father returns to judge your life on Earth. Not one of you is good and each of you will be in tears. But the Lord is merciful. He is slow to anger. He is quick to forgive. Count your lucky stars for that all you sinners and evil doers! Amen.

When I put it all together, my grand conclusion is: It is counterintuitive, the whole idea of "letting them see you cry"; grown, tough women can cry. Sometimes, it is exactly what needs to happen to get your way. Just be judicious about it.

Paris, Everest, Joy and Cake

Thirty five
A trip to Paris

At 35, I ran off to Paris toting a knapsack. I was reeling after the bust up of a particularly toxic relationship with the ultimate double-crossing Mr. Wrong, whom I like to call "the Mongoose." I had $1,000 and I decided to go to Paris to reinvent myself and marry a Frenchman. Tooooo funny.

First of all, damn fool that I was I cannot speak French. Second of all, damn fool that I was, I did not know a single soul in Paris. Third of all, damn fool that I was, I had only USD $400 spending money (about 350 Euros) after I purchased the airline ticket. Make a long story short, the damn fool that I was found a cheap room at a hostel in the Fourteenth Arrondissement populated by 18 year old college students, and an off-the-books job babysitting a five year old girl whose name I think was Lea (the cutest little thing) in Malakoff (a suburb of Paris). But I wasn't enjoying Paris. I was too distracted to focus on anything. I was too broke to eat at the cafes and subsisted on bread, cheese and goat milk. I could not afford day trips to Provence or Chartres or a day pass to the Louvre or entrance to any of the world famous museums. I was just bumming around Paris like a teenager, with no money; walking down the Champs Elysees and the other boulevards with ashy skin and nappy hair. When I got tired of walking I would sit in a park, like the Tuileries, or the Luxemburg Gardens and watch all the lovers go by. It was pretty sad.

I beat around Paris in a daze for a few months, a zombie, before I realized that what I was doing with my life was BS and a total waste of time for a woman my age. I was not a bloody poet. I was not a bloody writer. I was not the daughter of well-to-do Americans. I was not a pretty young thing who was killing a summer in Paris. What was I doing in Paris? I was a grown woman and I had a life back home which needed to be fixed. I had to return home to clean up my mess and get my life together! I was back to the States in a matter of months. I hit the pavement running and haven't been back to Paris since.

It saddens me that after three trips to Paris, I still cannot say I ever "enjoyed" Paris. It's just one of those strange things. I would so love to go again one more time; this time with the love of my life, and with enough time and money to do it justice rather than living there as an illegal alien, which is not fun. Always better to go with some cash, stay at a nice place, like the Hotel Crillon, and experience Paris the way it was meant to be experienced: as a capital of romance, culture, cuisine and history. Paris is truly a great city for grown ups. Next to New York, it is probably the most amazing city in the World. Every forty year old should go at least once. But properly. When your head is straight and you have the money to really enjoy the city the way it should be enjoyed.

If I talked to Oprah, Donald Trump and Jesus I think they would say the following:

Oprah: I remember one year I went to Paris and this world famous store refused to let me in. I was appalled but it turns out that they were in the midst of closing for the day or something like that. They did call the Oprah Show and apologized so all is forgiven. I say, why hold a grudge? It gets in the way of living your best life. But like everybody else, I love Paris. I love New York too, and many other Cities. But I have to say my favorite city is Chicago.

Donald Trump: My favorite city is right here in New York. My favorite place in New York is my home, Trump Tower. People come from all over the world to see Trump Tower. It's a real tourist attraction and that's because it's the best. There is nothing like it anywhere in the world. I am not a guy who likes to travel that much. Oh, I have a private jet. I can go anywhere I want to go in the world Buenos Aires, Hong Kong, United Emirates, Botswana, and Guam. But I prefer to be right here at home. Or at my place in Palm Beach. Do I like Paris? Sure, it's a nice place to visit. But I wouldn't want to live there.

Jesus: Paris is nice. New York is nice. Chicago is nice. But you should see my City! Amen.

When I put it all together my grand conclusion is: It is good to love what you have the best.

.

Thirty-six
Find your Everest and climb it

Each human being has aspirations and goals. It is the brave and the lucky who are able to accomplish all they set out to do in life all by the time they are forty. Forty is a big age but it is young if you can say you've already done everything in life that you wanted to do. Maybe too young. Surely there's one Everest left to climb? We all have many different Everests we would like to climb at different stages in our lives.

When I was younger, I had a whole different take on the concept of "luck" and "bravery." Who is really brave? Who is really lucky? Only those people who think they are. If one goes through life thinking, "I am scared, I can't do this," then chances are, they will not take may risks in life and will live a life of under achievement, and they will wake up one day, forty years old and the mountain would still be there taunting them. Too much caution can be as bad as being reckless. If one goes through life and believes that they are not "lucky" a lot of mishaps will come their way. It is easier to see that both bravery and luck, like most things in life, are personal choices. Anybody can choose to be brave or lucky, just by changing their mindset. Once we conquer our thinking, I think we begin to realize that the only thing to stop us from climbing our Everests, is us. It's not about having as many Everests as the Donald. For most people that would just be exhausting. It is about having goals and aspirations and setting out on your journey to achieve them, one by one, step by step. There is absolutely no reason why not, except fear.

When you get to be forty, you've got to stop being afraid. You just have to be braver. If not now, when? It is true that there are a lot of famous people did not get famous for what ever it is they got famous for till they were forty years old, or older. If you are a late bloomer like me, it is important to know that we are not alone we are not a dying breed. Many people peak long after forty. The thing is not to let fear be the reason you don't ever reach your peak. Don't let fear be a permanent killer of your dreams.

Mr. Trump is interesting; I read his books and I am inspired by him on many levels. This is a man who clearly had many Everests to climb and he climbed them all, and then some. But I was stunned when he wrote, "I am never satisfied. If I was I wouldn't be

Donald Trump." I cannot think in my little forty year old pea brain, what other Everests Donald Trump could have left to climb that would make him feel dissatisfied. What will make him satisfied, having the first hotel on the moon? What will he call it? Lunar Trump? Trump Galactic Hotel and Casino? Trump Moon Taj Mahal?

Obviously, this is a man who has infinite Everests to climb. And he even says that sometimes he feels like "Sisyphus who was condemned to push a boulder uphill for eternity." I find this instructive. First of all, I want success but I never want to feel condemned. But more important, whereas I thought that once we have climbed our own personal Everests, that we would naturally be overcome with an enormous sense of satisfaction, and peace, maybe that is not so. Maybe we only see more peaks across the valley, maybe we are all a little bit like Trump, maybe it is not in our nature to be satisfied. I certainly don't think God is ever satisfied. He keeps perfecting his craft. He keeps improving on perfection. He still works hard. I really see God as a guy who keeps working every single day. He never takes a day off. He never stops creating. He never has "enough." But then again, God is not limited to time and space the way Trump and the rest of us are. Somebody might want to clue in Mr. Trump—if they dare.

If I talked to Oprah, Donald Trump and Jesus I think they would say the following:

Oprah: I feel there is so much left for me to do. I so get it now. What I have been given is a gift. I have to find a way to make a difference; I feel my purpose is to make a difference in everybody's life. I feel I was meant to help everybody live their best life.

Donald Trump: First of all I'm not an outdoorsy kind of a guy. So you are not going to catch me mountain climbing. But there's always more to get and I want it. I wanted to be president but then I decided it wasn't worth my while. I still might run for mayor or governor of New York. I am certain I would be a much better governor that what's his face who shall remain nameless who said: "I don't want to bother the secretary." Can you believe this guy? Boy. So I may run for governor. We'll see. But I am never happy with the status quo. More is possible and I want it all. I am a creative guy. Why should I be satisfied with "enough" when I can have "all?" As for luck, you make your own luck. Luck is a result, it is an effect. You have to lay the ground work for luck to manifest. Every "lucky" person is an enterprising actor and a doer. You will hardly ever find a lucky person whose claim to fame is that they sat on their ass. Lucky people are lucky because they act. Even the people who win Mega Lotto took action. That's why they got lucky.

Jesus: Blessed are you who find your purpose in life, and live your life purposefully. Amen.

When I put it all together, my grand conclusion is: Be brave, be lucky.

Thirty-seven
The herd can be wrong

By forty, one should be better able to stand by one's convictions whatever they may be. When we are young we want to be like everybody else. We don't want to be different. It takes too much courage and confidence to be different. It is so much easier to be like everybody else. There is definitely safety in numbers. But when you get to be forty, you start to crave more individuality. You start to want to be one of a kind in the way you dress, live, speak, think, love. Sure, you still conform. We are creatures of conformity, we have to be. But to a large extent, you find ways to stand out from the herd, to be different, when you become a grown up.

Increasingly, it seems like everybody has to enjoy the same things or they will be seen as weird. It used to matter more to me that people didn't find me weird. Now it doesn't matter as much. I readily admit that I have never seen a single episode of American Idol, or Greys Anatomy, or any of the other super popular shows that everybody watches. Actually, I don't even have a television in my room. I don't have cable. I don't have an I-pod and I have no plans to get one. If it makes me weird so be it. It get my news on the internet.

There are many ways we try to conform in our youth. But I have come to learn that this does not necessarily set one on the right trajectory in one's life. This, in fact, can hold you back and keep you from living their best life. What is good for the goose is not necessarily good for the gander. As Donald Trump said, if he always did what others did, he would not own all the real estate he does today. He talks a lot about 40 Wall Street, which happens to be right next to New York Sports Club in the Financial District of Manhattan and this happens to be where I work out on occasion so I can tell you it's a gorgeous piece of real estate. He got this building because he didn't follow the herd, he followed his own instinct. And in the end, he got the building for free. There's a huge lesson in there somewhere.

If I talked to Oprah, Donald Trump and Jesus I think they would say the following:

Oprah: When I decided to endorse Obama people thought I was voting against Hilary Clinton. I wasn't. It would have been easier to vote for Hilary because she was more popular. But I didn't want to be a part of the herd. I had an opinion and I had a right to vote and I voted for the person who in my opinion was the better candidate. I wanted to see this country live its best life. I thought Obama was the best candidate who could help America "live" its best life. It didn't mean I thought Hilary wasn't good too. I just thought Obama was better. It was a vote for, not against. I decided to go against the herd.

Donald Trump: There's only one Donald Trump. I was born a leader. I lead the herd. It's not my fault. For some people it's the way it is. I don't have to work very hard at being a leader. It just fits me. I have always had a lot of energy. That's why my parents sent me to military school so that I could learn to conduct myself in a constructive, productive way. My parents raised all success stories. They are not stupid. They were very good parents. Then I put myself through Wharton for my college education. I was a good student and I took my education very seriously. But I was never going to be a part of a herd. I didn't spend all day and all night studying like all the other geniuses who, today, didn't make it. No, I was making deals when in college. I always wanted to be the best. I never wanted to be average or a part of the herd.

Jesus: Sometimes the herd is just wrong--trust me when I say this. Follow your heart. Do what you know is right. Amen.

When I put it all together my grand conclusion is: Do your own thing. Follow your heart. Don't be afraid to be different. Sometimes, embracing your difference is the first step to achieving greatness. Don't settle for mediocrity. Do the right thing.

Thirty-eight
Destroy the weakling to get to the lion

It is puzzling how violent nature can be. I see God as almost this pacifist and then I watch National Geographic and get horrified at how much violence there is in the animal kingdom. It gives former President Bill Clinton's facial expressions during the Democratic Primaries, after Senator Clinton lost the Iowa caucus, perspective. Remember that violent scowl? He looked like an angry lion stirred from slumber and looking for the culprit. Had he found Senator Obama, the former President might have had him for appetizer and might have enjoyed tearing flesh from bone with his bared, snarled teeth. It was like, "Don't mess with a sleeping lion or his wife!"

But seriously. Animals destroy and kill other animals in nature and all this blood shed leaves me traumatized and sometimes outraged. However, entire ecosystems would cease to exist without this violence and the resulting destruction. If one species does not kill, eat or destroy the other, they could all become extinct over time. Everything is so interconnected. It makes me wonder if there might be a "divine" purpose to war, other than to confirm that we really are nothing but senseless, primitive animals.

This natural inclination to destroy suggests, that as a product of nature, humans must destroy not only to survive, but to advance to the next level. But what is it okay to destroy? Do we have carte blanche to destroy anything in our paths so long as our objective is survival?

Some of us would prefer to not have to destroy anything at all. Of course, that may be a big part of our problem, as late bloomers, a big part of why we are behind the pack: We're too nice! We do not have the killer instinct that is needed in order to win, to get what we want and deserve. Whose fault is that? I, personally, always over-sympathize with the opponent, put myself in their shoes. And guess what invariably happens? I get eaten--by the very people I was sympathizing with. That's what. I could never have survived on the Apprentice. Nor could I have ever run for political office.

It is not just the animals that are violent and that destroy. Nature is full of other forms of destruction. There are things like famines, diseases, pestilence, earthquakes, tornadoes, tsunamis, lightening, floods, hurricanes, all sorts of "natural" disasters that are totally violent and that destroy many people and things. Why? What is the lesson? What is the purpose? Is this all just a part of the "perfect" design? And how can I apply this fact to my life to help myself stop being a late bloomer? Well, after animals kill, something is dead; no more. But after any other "natural disaster," there is usually calm, there is renewal, there is a rainbow. So, some forms of "destruction" are necessary so that life can become calmer and renewed. There is no rainbow without a storm—sometimes the more the destructive the storm, the more brilliant the rainbow.

When I look back on my youth, I see a lot of violence and destruction. Some of the mistakes I have made have been unbelievably destructive to my emotional state at the time I made them. I have caused more violence to my peace with some of the bad choices I have made than any tsunami or earthquake could have done. My self-inflicted wounds could easily have killed me, just in the same way as animals in the jungle easily kill other animals. Sometimes I inflicted the wound but I gave the weapon to someone else. But somehow, I am stronger today than I was in my youth. Maybe there are things within ourselves that must first be destroyed before we can really reach calm, before we can have our rainbows? Maybe we have to kill the weakling in order to get to the lion within?

If I talked to Oprah, Donald Trump and Jesus I think they would say the following:

Oprah: This is a very interesting theory. Maybe in order to live our best life we have to destroy something. I don't know. Caller, you say what?

Donald: I am not big into this hocus pocus mumbo jumbo about rainbows and mean girls going to Heaven. But I do believe that nature is the most powerful force and I do not mess with nature because "nature will always win." As a business man, I see people act like animals all the time. I have said in my books that "at least the lion kills for food. We kill for the thrill of the hunt." It has no purpose but it is great. I love a good fight. I like to hit them hard till they drop to their knees crying for their mama. I swear there's nothing like seeing a big tough guy on his knees crying for his mama. I saw a lot of tough guys crying for their mama to put a pacifier in their mouths during the nineties when real estate went belly up in New York. Ha Ha Ha. It was pretty funny. I laughed so hard I thought it was raining.

Jesus: The Lord thy God is mysterious his wonders to behold. Do not try to understand the ways of the Lord. Amen.

When I put it all together my grand conclusion is: Get tough.

Thirty-nine
Your Joy is your Job

How many times do you hear that it is your job to make yourself happy? It's not your parent's job, it's not your husband's job, it's not your children's job, it's not your boss's job; it is not your friends' job. It's your job to make yourself happy. It is your job to give yourself joy. How many times do you have to hear it before it sinks in? How about 40 years? You have to hear this for forty years before it hits you like a rocket. IT IS MY JOB TO MAKE MYSELF HAPPY. IT IS MY JOB TO FILL MYSELF WITH JOY.

Happiness is a very elusive thing. What is happiness? How does one measure it? Can one ever be happy and not know? Is it really true that only you can make yourself happy? Is it really true that happiness is a choice? What are the ingredients of happiness? How long do you have to bake it in order for it to be ready for consumption? Is happiness measurable? Is it transferable? Is it visible? What color is happiness? What are its dimensions?

In my twenties, I tried a weird experiment. I decided I was going to be happy. It was just an experiment. I wanted to see what would happen if I simply *decided* to be happy. So armed with nothing except my decision which I basically made in the wind, I became happy. Just like that. I used to laugh a lot, but now I was a hyena. I smiled all the time. But now I was grinning like a complete fool. I greeted everyone with a big smile, and lots of bubble. It really became this personal phenomenon; this transformation and metamorphosis. The most beautiful part of it was, I was happy just because. It didn't take anything. Like magic, my outlook on life changed. I became "deliriously" filled up with joy for no apparent reason. My thoughts of happiness really began to have what I can only describe as a narcotic effect. I guess that is what euphoria is. I was so high with this strange emotion that I started to even irritate my friends. One friend said: keep it up and somebody is going to pop your bubble! She was right.

It was the strangest thing, really. The happier I got, the more people seemed to hate me. At first, I couldn't believe it. I couldn't believe that people would be annoyed and resentful just because I was happy. I wanted to scream: I have no money. I have no man. I have no real estate. I have nothing. I am just happy just because. But I didn't dare. I knew nobody wanted to hear it. All that mattered was I was walking around the place being bubbly and smiling and laughing and charming and *they thought* I was happy. Most people were having none of it. They wanted to squat me like a bug. I quickly learned that happiness could be dangerous. It meant people would start gunning for me, to take me down, to reduce me to tears and make me feel bad—which they did.

    I can't help remembering when Tom Cruise jumped on Oprah's couch declaring his love for Katie Holmes. It seemed the whole world turned on him and pelted him with rocks. It was as if he had done something terrible, like moon the cameras bare-bottomed, or hit his wife, or called the Pope a degenerate. I felt bad for him. He might have fared better if he had jumped on the couch after telling the audience he had kicked a coke habit, or some other prurient thing. He might have gotten a standing ovation for his couch dance in that case. Poor Tom. The poor guy was just feeling deliriously, crazily happy about a simple thing called LOVE and he shared it; for that, he nearly got his ass crucified. For that, his career was almost destroyed. And why? Because the people who were judging him had never experienced that kind of love—the kind of love that would make a mega movie star and multi-millionaire act like a fool on Oprah. I don't blame people because I have never had that kind of love either. But I understand Tom Cruise. I understand that moment. He was just happy and excited and filled up with joy. It really is as simple as that.

Most people are not happy. I hate to say it but it's true. People are richer, thinner and healthier than they have ever been. But they are not happier. And they have no appreciation for happy people. They don't appreciate happiness in others because they don't understand how to be happy themselves. They keep looking for outside stimuli. They don't see the futility of looking for happiness outside of themselves. People are convinced they will never *find* happiness. So they settle on some other emotion. They do drugs to forget their misery. They live in a place called "Prozac Nation." They live a life of debauchery and gross excess. They are rich, beautiful and young, yet they stumble around in a drunken stupor on the streets without shirts, without drawers. They revel in the misfortunes of others. They put others down for no reason, other than to try to feel better—although they never feel better. They are empty inside. There is no true happiness in making others miserable. None of us can nurture or appreciate happiness in others unless and until we can appreciate and achieve it for ourselves.

Most people don't get that it's a matter of making the decision to be happy. It's about choosing to be happy. But Tom and I learned the hard way, better to practice happiness quietly, under the radar. No need to announce it on a bullhorn or jump on a couch. No need to shine your happiness too bright. Somebody could take a crow bar to your bulb.

If I talked to Oprah, Donald Trump and Jesus I think they would say the following:

Oprah: Here Here. One of the fundamental precepts of living your best life is realizing that your happiness is your choice, and your decision. You cannot be happy unless you think you are happy. You cannot find happiness unless you choose to be so.

Donald: Am I happy? I don't know. That's a deep question. I have never really thought about it. I would say I am successful. I would say I possess a lot of things. I am abundant. I am proud of a lot of things, like my children, my wife, my ex-wives, and my work. Yet, I don't know if I would say that I am happy. That seems kind of girlish.

Jesus: Happiness is peace. Happiness is God. Amen

When I put it all together, my grand conclusion is: Don't worry be happy; but don't jump on Oprah's couch unless it's in celebration of your sobriety or release from prison, or rehab because people will call you c.r.a.z.y and your career could be caput.

Forty
Eat your cake and have it too (don't be bulimic)

I love cake. It was never completely clear to me what "have your cake and eat it too," means. Or did they mean "eat your cake and have it too?" Either way you slice it, I don't get it. What else are you to do with cake except eat it? Whoever came up with that must have been a bulimic Mommy Dearest.

I think getting to forty is so fabulous and magnificent! It is such an accomplishment for me. It calls for a celebration that involves lots of cake. Getting to forty and not dying from all the brutal lessons and pain, at least for me, means hogging out on cake. I can't believe I lived to talk about it. I really can't.

One must affirmatively choose to have one's cake in life; however, not only must one eat it when given a chance, but one must also enjoy how it feels going down, and one must savor it going down, and one must let it stay down and not rob oneself of the pleasure by regurgitating.

Cake is your reward! Chew the damn thing with great satisfaction, swallow, and let it digest. Do not throw it back up. Do not allow yourself to think you don't deserve to have your cake and eat it. Do you remember what it took to get here? How can you allow some food addict to take away the pleasure that only comes from eating cake by telling you to have your cake but not to eat it?

I believe the saying, "to everything there is a season; and a time to every purpose under Heaven." There's a time to cry, a time to laugh, a time to diet, a time to eat cake. There's a time for a small cake and a time for a big cake. There's a time to have just one slice and share it with company, and a time to eat the whole thing by your self.

I certainly don't believe you should subsist on just cake, don't misunderstand. That is very fattening and can get sickening very quickly. Too much cake is not good and will dull your pleasure the next time around. Then you won't want cake when the occasion calls for cake. So be sparing in your cake splurges. But by forty, you know your cake moments. You know when you need to acknowledge yourself even if no one else notices you've had a big moment. It is not all the time that others will know when you deserve a reward, by the way. But it is very important that you know yourself and acknowledge yourself and eat your cake.

If I talked to Oprah, Donald Trump and Jesus I think they would say the following:

Oprah: Live your best life! Sometimes we have to eat cake even though we know just to look at it adds ten pounds to the hips! Isn't that the truth ladies? Over the holidays, I confess I had me some sweet potato pie. I love Sweet potato pie. My best friend Gayle, she loves cake. Just give her a man and some cake and she's good to go. But you know what? Sometimes, it's okay. So long as it's not an addiction its okay. Sometimes you have to have your cake and eat it.

Donald Trump: I almost never eat cake. A woman can have cake if she has a body that can accommodate it.

Jesus: Eat, drink and be merry. The kingdom of God is at hand. Amen.

When I put it all together, my grand conclusion is: have your cake. You earned it. Boy, did you earn it. How? Well, you lived to talk about it.

To sum it all up

So I have learned a lot by writing this book. I have taught myself through this internal dialogue and hopefully if you read the book from cover to cover, something I said inspired you too.

I don't know about you but I'm not taking this late bloomer thing lying down anymore. Damn straight I'm not. I have the tools to change the course of my life. I've learned a lot of lessons. Oprah, Donald and Jesus are very clear in setting their example. I have the tools. There is no excuse for me to continue the current trajectory.

The point is to act with purpose or not act at all. The point is to act with Faith; practice gratitude. The point is to think big. The point is one must impose one's will upon oneself; worry about oneself while caring about the world; but "not concerning oneself with what anybody else is doing." It's a delicate balance but it must be, and can be done. The point is to remember that everybody out there is not nice. Everybody out there does not have good intentions. Some people just want to blow your best laid plans to smithereens just for kicks, to get a good laugh. One cannot afford to continue to be naive if one wants to get on track and start to bloom. It is critical that one learns to watch one's back, and protect one's stuff. It is critical that one gets kinetic and stop being so potential. It is critical that one gets tough, unleash that inner lion.

Come on, let's do it together. Let's get brave...

See how we have achieved so many of our dreams? See how we have climbed so many our Everests in such a short space of time?

How did this all happen? It is simple: we started to think like heavy-hitters instead of like a little mice. We learned from our mistakes, and we applied the lessons to our life. We created the life we wanted. We sculpted the sculpture that we wanted. We did not give up on ourselves and on the magic and mystery of the Universe. We did not give up on the dream. We knew everything was in the process of manifesting, that it was just a matter of time. We never lost hope. We never thought, "I'm a failure" just because we took a while longer to bloom. We gave the Invisible its due.

Look at all that has happened. Our careers are flourishing. We are in well-adjusted relationships. We are financially and spiritually abundant. We feel in sync and in balance. It is feeling like success. I know I am feeling success coming on. I know my success is about to manifest. I wish the same for you. Thank you Oprah! Thank you Donald! Thank you Jesus!!!

Appendix

Forty Grand Conclusions about how to turn a midlife crisis on its exquisite nose as taken from the "masters":

1. If you ask for something, even if it is far fetched and beyond your imagination, you might get it; so be careful what you

ask for. Also, never take the bus for 19 hours trips across States—that's a joke. And while you're at it, learn to control your mother! (Shhh. Don't tell my mother I said this.)

2. The size of a person's best life is directly correlated to how he or she thinks. Before one can kick ass, one has to think she can kick ass. One has to think big. The Alpha and the Omega is vast. If we all only think as big as a small fraction of that, our thoughts will be enormous. Then the size of our lives will start to correspond to the enormity of our thoughts.

3. Abundance is a limitless resource and our "best life" is a life of abundance; our "best life" is for us to create; We create our abundance with the grace of God (we create our lack of

abundance too, when we fail to understand God); God is abundant and wants every person to be abundant; He expects those who are abundant to help those who are not.

4. A person's best life is a life that expands and does not remain static; a person's best life is one that keeps getting better. Never skimp on your creativity; always have faith that you can create the life you want. Always keep busy; never stop trying to reach your peak. Never be satisfied with less than your best.

5. Where money is concerned, it is important to keep things in perspective; there is more to life than just money. That doesn't mean money is not critically important. So long as

we have life, money will be critically important. Also, everyone should be educated about money, like any other subject, in school. That way, people can start to make good, sound, financial decisions and not plummet into a financial landmine through ignorant decision-making and rash behavior. Take responsibility for your behavior with respect to money. Yet, it is foolish to think that money is all that there is. In the end, we will not be judged by how much money was in our bank accounts.

6. Respect money; value money enough not to waste it on nonsense, lest it runs out and leave you broke.

7. Mistakes come from bad judgment; but mistakes teach us important life lessons. These lessons save us from bigger screw ups later down the road. It doesn't make sense to dwell on mistakes, however, only to learn from them and apply them in the future; at the same time, some mistakes are avoidable. If we do the right thing from the very start we'll have a whole lot less regrets to talk about in the future.

8. There comes a time in every person's life when they have to grow up and put away their childish nonsense. I, personally, can't run a billion dollar business if I'm a kid—unless I am a Trump—which I'm not. Therefore, for that and other reasons, it is imperative that I mature emotionally and not just chronologically. That's probably true for you too?

9. No matter how smart we may think we are, we need to write things down to keep on top of it all; our best life is organized, planned (to some extent) and free from chaos.

10. Nothing is guaranteed. Here today, gone tomorrow. A person's best life means that they make a point of enjoying each day, each moment. It means they squeeze as much living as they can into every moment. It doesn't have to be loud and draw attention. One can make a quiet splash (or a loud splash) if one is so inclined. Life is short. Live and let live.

11. Stand your ground and defend yourself; but stop short of hurting others without a good reason. If you hurt others without cause then apologize. Mr. Trump might say that your best life means being unapologetically tough. It is a lot easier on the heart to go a little softer on some people, some of the time.

12. While you have life, do the best you can to live as well as you can; but live a life of love—for others and for yourself; and while you're at it, kick some ass too.

13. You can only live *your* best life. Competition could be overrated if it is taken to an extreme. Sure it fuels business but life is not all business. Life is not "the Apprentice." Life

is not competitive golf. Look, would I be the worse soccer mom if I ever had kids? Of course. But it doesn't make it right and it doesn't make it fulfilling. Our best lives is a happy dose of balance, abundance, consideration for others, love for ourselves and a spiritual connection.

14. One ought to find a cause to care about and do it. One ought to give a fig. It doesn't have to be huge. Maybe we can start by not wasting so much paper. Or taking shorter showers. Or carpooling sometimes.

15. Be careful in the choices you make. Love is too important to be treated lightly.

16. A vajayjay is a priced possession.

17. Never give up hope. Things can change. All you have to do is seek change and it will happen. But be specific about what you are searching for. Don't confuse the Universe.

18. Breasts are just flesh; but they do look a lot better when they are surgically enhanced and today's men seem to go for gravity-defying fake ones than sagging real ones, don't they? Oprah is rich enough that she doesn't care what anybody thinks about her breasts. If we were all as rich as Oprah, we wouldn't have to think about lifting our breasts.

19. It's tough to be a woman. But studies show that more men get sex change operations to become women than the other way around; so, it must also be more fun to be a woman, in spite of the challenges.

20. Wear Camouflage.

21. Be a good friend and only keep good friends.

22. It is possible to have a healthy friendship that does not involve envy and competition; at the same time, sometimes friends are not there for you when you expect them to be. Be big enough to forgive them most of the time; if what they did

is egregious however Mr. Trump makes it clear that you can blast them in your books and never talk to them again.

23. There are no rules for dressing so long as one wears underwear in public and so long as one respects oneself and one's body and not pull a Britney Spears; that's not a good look even if you're under twenty-five.

24. Unless you have multiple houses like Oprah, you don't need 200 pairs of shoes. But you can indulge yourself so long as you take care of the important things first—like getting rental real estate.

25. Be nice. Don't say bad things about people. If they say bad things about you and it potentially damages your reputation, call them on it, even if you have to do it publicly. If it is possible to ignore bullies who try to sully your name or reputation without cause, ignore them. If you can't, let them have it. But the rule "if you can't say something nice don't say anything," is a good rule.

26. Better just to stay healthy if at all possible so as to avoid the headache of fixing your broken health—that is potentially perilous.

27. In your prayers it is important to ask not only for financial abundance, but abundantly good health too—which is more important than all the money in the world.

28. Everything has a price. If you can't pay the price, think twice before getting the merchandise. (But don't suffer on a job. Too much of our lives are spent at work. One should be happy at work. Just don't quit till you get another one cause you may go bankrupt.)

29. It is a woman's prerogative to change her mind, but it may not be in her best interest to be so capricious all the time.

30. Don't nag. But ask the life genie for what you want and you will receive it. Just make sure you really want it.

31. Don't get bogged down by problems because it gets in the way of living your best life. The more problems you can solve, the more valuable you will be to yourself and others. When the going gets tough, a little prayer can't hurt. "Grow yourself to be bigger than the problems."

32. Root yourself in good soil in order to get good fruits.

33. God doesn't know what a half full glass is and no one should be satisfied with a half full glass if it is possible to have a full glass.

34. It is counterintuitive, the whole idea of "letting them see you cry"; but grown, tough women can and do cry. Sometimes, it is exactly what needs to happen to get your way. Just be judicious about it.

35. 35. It is good to love what you have, the best.

36. 36. Be brave, be lucky

37. Do your own thing. Follow your heart. Don't be afraid to be different. Sometimes, embracing your difference is the first step to achieving greatness. Don't settle for mediocrity. Try to do the right thing as often as you can.

38. Get tough.

39. Don't worry be happy; but don't jump on Oprah's couch unless it's in celebration of your sobriety or release from prison, or successful completion of this year's stint in rehab because people will call you c.r.a.z.y and your career could be caput.

40. Have your cake. Eat your cake. You earned it. Boy, did you earn it. How? Well, you lived to talk about it.

Bibliography

On Being 40

How to Survive Your 40th Birthday: The Complete Guide to Getting the Care You Need--and Avoiding the Problems You Don't, by Bill Dodds.

>MeadowBrook 1990. "How to Survive Your 40th Birthday is a perfect gift for thirty-nine-year-olds dreading the Big Four 40. It provides reassurance that there's more to life after forty: old age and death. And it's chock fun of off-the-wall advice that can come in very handy when you turn forty."

The big 40! by Joshua Albertson. Crown 2004. "Tells you how to celebrate this landmark birthday and the decade that follows."

You Know you are 40 when... by Ann Hodgman and Patricia Marx.

Broadway. 2005. "Whether you've just found your first gray hair or are peering at your midlife crisis this book will tickle your funny bone."

What you don't know about turning 40: A funny Birthday quiz, by Bill Dodds and Bruce Lansky. MeadowBrook 2006. "This over-the-hill birthday gift is a pop quiz with 101 questions (complete with humorous answers) that is sure to enliven any 40th birthday party. Steve Mark's 18 b/w illustrations make the book fun to read after the party, as well."

On Women Turning Forty: Coming Into Our Fullness, by Cathleen Rountree. Crossing Press 1991 "This book offers thoughtful, well-written essays by a diverse group of women who share a focus on interior, intentional living and have significantly progressed toward self-actualization."

Turning 40: Wit, Wisdom, and Wining, by William Klingaman. Amazon Remainders Account 1992. "On the back page was this wonderful message: 'Some of us age like old wine. Others don't get older, they get sharper. The idea is to think of your 40th birthday as the beginning of the rest of your life. This is the book that delivers the sure-fire, feel-great-about-it attitude you need - good advice, good laughs, & best of all, lots of good company.'"

Forty things to Do When You Turn Forty: Forty Experts on the Subject of Turning Forty by

Ronnie Sellers. Sellers Publishing 2007. "Forty Things To Do When You Turn Forty is a collection of essays that speaks to the reader who has or will soon turn 40. Forty essayists from all walks of life have written on the subject of turning 40; covering issues that are practical, on subjects like health care, fitness, finance, and business, and essays that are reflective, whimsical, or reassuring or just plain laugh-out-loud funny. All royalties will be donated to cancer research."

1003 Great Things About Getting Older by Lisa Birnbach. Andrews McMeel 1997.

The Right Side of Forty: Celebrating Timeless Women, by Patricia Martin. Conari Press 1997

"The right side is definitely inspiring. I am one of the women in the book and found myself inspired by reading about and meeting some of the other women as well as patty and leif!! It should give anyone dreading turning forty an incentive to know that life just begins!!"

Forty and Stuck in the Middle, by Jenine Weyrauch. PerVict Body 2003. "A great and passionate life doesn't happen by chance, it happens by choice. Take a deeper look at who you are, and who it is that you want to become. Start being "An Achiever" of great things and make your life happen, by getting "un-stuck," and moving forward to a more positive and productive life ... 'A Journey of Your Greatness.'"

Forty Reasons Why life is More fun after the Big 40 by Liz Curtis Higgs.

Thomas Nelson Publishers 1997.

On Thinking Big

Think Big and Kick Ass by Donald Trump. Collins 2007. "These strategies are proven and attested to by those who've learned to think BIG from Donald Trump and found success in their own lives. Bill Zanker used Donald's strategies to grow the revenues of The Learning Annex twenty times in under three years. Both of them have been down and out, and know what it's like to feel the whole world's against you—and both have risen to dizzying heights of success by thinking BIG and kicking ass! It is an attitude that can be easily learned."

The Millionaire Next Door by, Thomas Stanley and William Danko. Pocket 2000. "Stanley and Danko mercilessly show how wealth takes sacrifice, discipline, and hard work, qualities that are positively discouraged by our high-consumption society."

Think Like a Billionaire, Donald Trump. Ballantine 2004. Trump will take you behind the scenes, from the end of season one and into season two, with insights into the making and the meaning of TV's hottest show. As Donald Trump proves, getting rich is easy. *Staying* rich is harder. Your chances are better, and you'll have more fun, if you think like a billionaire. This is the book that will help you make a real difference in your life."

The Courage to Be Rich, Suze Orman. Riverhead Books 1999. "There is no more persuasive, compelling and honest a financial teacher today than Suze Orman. Building on the rock-solid foundation of her earlier lessons, The courage to be Rich is in every sense higher education on matters of vital importance to us all."

The Automatic Millionaire, David Bach. Broadway Books 2004.

"Despite its sensational title, David Bach's *The Automatic Millionaire: A Powerful One-Step Plan to Live and Finish Rich* is not a get-rich-quick guide. Rather, the book is a straightforward march through common-sense personal financial planning that suggests readers "automate" their contributions to retirement and investment vehicles. Bach, in fact, calls his model the "tortoise approach" to becoming wealthy by retirement age."

The Guide to Becoming Rich, Robert Kiosk. Business Plus 2003.

"The real trick to building personal wealth is learning how to transform 'bad debt' into 'good debt.' This quick-hitting book explains how-without having to cut up credit cards. This is the eighth book in the phenomenally successful Rich Dad series. This book was originally published as an e-book and now joins the Rich Dad series in trade paperback format."

Before you Quit Your Job, Robert Kiyosaki. Business Plus 2005.

"Expressing the same philosophy he espouses in his RICH DAD POOR DAD series, Kiyosaki presents his plan for would-be entrepreneurs in a clear and organized manner."

How to Be Rich, Donald Trump. Ballantine 2004. "Trump appears comfortable with himself, and he even makes light of potentially touchy subjects, such as his hair: "My hair is one hundred percent mine. No animals have been harmed in the creation of my hairstyle."

The Science of Being Rich, Wallace D. Wattles. Tarcher 2007. "In his

> seventeen short, straight-to-the-point chapters, Wattles shows how to use this idea, how to overcome barriers to its application, and how work with very direct methods that awaken it in your life. He further explains how creation and not competition is the hidden key to wealth attraction, and how your power to get rich uplifts everyone around you."

Think and Grow Rich, Napoleon Hill. Tarcher 2005. "The bestselling success book of all time is updated and revised with contemporary ideas and examples."

The Secret, Rhonda Byrne. Atria Books 2006.

Secret of a Millionaire Mind, by T Harv Eker. Collins 2005. "In rat-a-tat, 'Let me explain" seminar-speak, Eker asks readers to think back to their childhoods and pick apart the lessons they passively absorbed from parents and others about money. With such psychological nuggets as "Rich people focus on opportunities/ Poor people focus on obstacles,' Eker puts a positive spin on stereotypes, arguing that poverty begins, or rather, is allowed to continue, in one's imagination first, with actual material life becoming a self-fulfilling prophecy."

The Weekend Millionaire's Secrets to Investing in Real Estate, by Mike Summey and Roger Dawson. McGraw Hill 2003. "You don't have to be independently wealthy or a tycoon to get started in real estate. This step-by-step guide shows you how to look beyond price to discover the true value of an investment property. It gives you a long-term strategy, based on sound market principles, to leverage this value to create a substantial cash flow *without* major capital investment."

Getting Rich Your Own Way, by Brian Tracy. Wiley 2006. "The strategies, techniques, and methods for achieving financial independence practiced by more than 95 percent of Americans who go from rags to riches in one generation– from the author of the BusinessWeek bestseller Create Your Own Future."

On Living Your Best Life and creating havoc

Fantastic Over 40: The Savvy Woman's Guide to her Best Season of Life, by Pam Farrel. Harvest Publishers 2007.

>"A conversation with baby boomer women who desire life enhancing resources."

How not to look Old: Fast and Effortless Ways to Look 10 Years Younger 10 Pounds Lighter, 10 Times Better, by Charla Krupp
>SpringBoard Press, 2007. A beauty and style bible for every woman.

The Celestine Prophesy, Bantam Books, 1996.

Life's Little Emergencies, Emme and Natasha Stoynoff. St. Martin's Press 2003. "In this frank, practical and hilarious guide to getting through life's everyday emergencies, Emme is our navigator. Her insider's eye and priceless connections will help you solve the dilemmas that come your way."

Shambhala, The Sacred Path of the Warrior, Chogyam Trungpa.

> Shambhala Productions, 1978. "In this practical guide to enlightened living, Chogyam Trungpa offers an inspiring vision for our time, based on the figure of the sacred warrior. In ancient times, the warrior learned to master the challenges of life, both on and off the battlefield."

40 Over 40: 40 Things Every Woman Over 40 Needs to Know About Getting Dressed by Brenda Reiten Kinsel and Jenny M. Phillips.

> Wildcat Canyon Press 2000. ("Turn dressing into an opportunity.")

How to Behave, by Caroline Tiger Quirk Books, 2003. "A guide to modern manners for the socially challenged."

Living Longer Stronger: The 6 Week Plan to Enhance and Extend Your Years Over 40 by Ellington Darden. Berkly Publishing Group 1995. "A book for middle age men on the virtues of strength training."

The Ten Smartest Decisions A Woman can Make Before 40 by Tina B. Tessina and Elizabeth Friar Williams. Health Communications 1998. "Find out how to lead your life and create the life you want by making fundamental choices."

Forty Days to your Best Life for Single Mothers, by Lora Schrock. Honor Books 2006. "No matter their race or background single mothers everywhere share a common purpose to raise healthy, happy, well adjusted children."

Your Best Life Now Study Guide: 7 Steps to living your full potential by

> Joel Osteen. Faithworks 2005. "Discussion questions, relevant scripture and insightful narratives to inspire readers to greatness."

On Health over 40

The Real Age Makeover by Michael F. Roizen. Collins: 2004. ("whether

> talking about stress, diet or disease, Roizen offers case examples and subtle and engaging strategies such as describing the role of living beyond your means in aging or the difference between "four-legged" and "no-leg fats."

Readers looking for a quick fix will benefit less than those who follow the recommendations that require focus and commitment.")

Dr. D's Handbook for Men Over 40: A guide to Health, Fitness, Living, and Loving in the Prime of Life by Peter Dorsen. Wiley: 1999. "A guide

for men to maximize the joys of life after 40."

When Your Hormones Go Haywire: Solutions for Women Over 40 by Pamela M. Smith Zondervan 2005. "Research designed to provide you with proven step by step solutions that will help you regain hormonal balance in midlife."

Fit over 40 for Dummies by Betsy Nagelsen McCormack and Mike Yorkey. For Dummies 2000. "Tennis pro Betsy Nagelson guides you to being fit over 40."

Thin over 40 by Gregory L. Jantz, PHD and Anne McMurray

> Signet 2004."Get a great new body and a positive new attitude through simple, daily assignments."

Fit not Fat at 40: The Shape -Up Plan that Balances Your Hormones, Boosts Your Metabolism, and fights Female Fat in Your Forties and Beyond, by Editors Prevention Health Book for Women. Rodale Books

> 2002. A weight loss guide for women over 40

Women's Health Over 40, What Your Should Know by Caroline J.

> Bohme. Wiley-Blackwell 2001. "Easy to read info about breast cancer, osteoporosis, heart disease and other health issue of women over 40."

Running and Walking for women over 40 by Kathrine Switzer. St.

Martins Press 1998. "How to transform your life and get fit running and walking."

On Family, Relationships and Sex

First Baby after 30...or 40: What to Expect When you're 30 Something or More by Dr. Penny Stanway. Orion Publishing 1999. "Pros can and

cons about having a first child later in life and how to avoid

or minimize potential problem."

But I don't feel too old to be a mommy!: The Complete Sourcebook for Starting (and Re-Starting) Motherhood Beyond 35 and After 40 by

Doreen Nagle. HCI 2002. "Written for women who have fears and doubts about motherhood after 35 and beyond 40. Supportive and realistic info."

Satisfaction: The Art of the Female Orgasm, by Kim Cattrall and Mark Levinson. New York: Warner Books, 2002

Wanna Know why You're still single? Dating for 30, 40, and 50 Somethings, by Joseph Kandel. Bridgeway Books 2007. "An eye-opener for both women and men and offers a unique, frank, and humorous look into why so many people are single. Joseph Kandel offers real-life examples from years of dating, wonderful relationships, and interviews with real people."

Cruising and Bruising in Cyberspace: A Guide to Online Dating After 40 by F. Ludwig, PhD. BookSurge Publishing 2007. "At last here is a

> guide for persons over 40 who are considering or participating in online dating and wish to maximize their positive results."

Laws of the Jungle: Dating for Women over 40, Gloria MacDonald and

> Thelma Beam. WAM Publishing 2007. "A fun, frank observation of the pitfalls facing middle age women looking

for

> relationships in an increasingly youth obsessed world."

Over 40 and Dating: The Thunder Years, by Jace Michaels. Inkwater

Press 2005. "The first part of a 2 part series of Jacie Michaels going on the adventure of a lifetime. After all, she's over 40 and dating. Let the storm roll on."

40 Unforgettable Dates with Your Mate by Barbara Rosberg. Tindale House Publishers 2002. "Forty fun and romantic dates to meet your spouse's love needs."

How Not to Stay Single After 40: the Secret to Finding Passion, Love, and Fulfillment--At Last, by Nita Tucker. Three Rivers Press 2002.

"This results-oriented book teaches you that wanting a relationship is nothing to be ashamed of, that staying in a dead-end relationship will keep you from finding a thriving one, that there are simple and effective ways to increase the odds of meeting the right kind of people, and that you're a good catch and shouldn't hide it."

Middle Aged and Dating Again by Tom Blake. Morris Publishing 1997.

"Blake advises mature singles to get out and meet people at night classes, concerts, church and community volunteer activities." He says, Develop new interests or rejuvenate old ones.' ...network with friends, co-workers and others. Ask them, Do you know of anyone I might enjoy meeting or going out with?' An insightful book."

10 Commandments of Dating by Ben Young. Thomas Nelson 1999.

"Are you tired of pouring time, energy and money into relationships that start off great and end with heartache? If so, you need *The Ten Commandments of Dating* to give you the hard-hitting, black-and-white, practical guidelines that will address your questions and frustrations about dating. This guide will help you keep your head in the search for the desire of your heart."

The Professional Bachelor Dating Guide: How to Exploit her Inner Psycho by Brett Tate. TPB Publishing, LLC 2007. "The Art of the Pickup involves analyzing your target, determine her values, beliefs and weaknesses, and role-playing her desires."

Stop Dating the Church: Fall in Love with the Family of God by Joshua Harris. *Stop Dating the Church* "reminds us that faith was never meant to be a solo pursuit. The church is the place God grows us, encourages us, and uses us best. Loving Jesus

Christ involves a passionate commitment to His church — around the world and down the street."

Dating an Older Man, by Jerome Albers. Trafford Publishing 2006. "The dating game is looked at honestly and humorously from many experiences. It discusses the best and worst places to meet desirable women. Bring back the fun women."

Sex Over 40: Completely Revised and Updated by Saul M. Rosenthal Amazon Remainders Account, 2000. Updated and revised guidebook to mature sexual health.

On Money & Miscellaneous

I'm in Debt, Over 40, with No Retirement Savings. HELP! by John L.

White. Bohannon Publishing. 2003. "A good mix of interesting biographical narrative and sound career and financial advise."

The Procrastinator's Guide to Financial Security: How Anyone Over 40 Can still build a Strong Portfolio--and retire comfortably, by David F

Teitelbaum AMACOM/American Management Association 2001. "The Procrastinator's Guide to Financial Security supplies a crash course in the fundamentals of money management. In a clear, straightforward way--but with a tone that stresses the urgency of the situation--the book helps readers develop the knowledge, skills, and discipline they need to secure a comfortable retirement."

40 Day Prosperity Plan by John Randolph Price. Hay House 2004.

"Timeless teaching from Ageless Wisdom, which reveal the truth about the Law of Abundance."

The Motley Fool's Money After 40: Building Wealth for a Better Life, by David Gardner and Tom Gardner. Fireside 2006.

"Co-founders of The Motley Fool financial education company, the Gardner brothers have built an empire out of their ability to make matters of personal finance so simple that any "fool" can learn to sort through them with a sense of confidence. Four of their last 10 books have been bestsellers; their latest offers comprehensive advice on the issues faced by the over-40 set, shared in their typically irreverent, blunt and highly informative way."

Your Credit Score by Liz Pulliam Weston. Prentice Hall 2005. "A complete action plan for improving your credit score—starting today! Information that could save you thousands on credit and insurance…even helps you get your next job."

On Career Issues

Finding the right Next Job When You're Over 40: A step by Step Real

Life Handbook for Making all the Right Moves in Today's Job Market,

by O.E. Unser. Forty-Something Plus 1995.

Success Over 40 by Mason Marie Baker. Writers Club Press 2000.

Over 40 and Looking for work? A Guide for the Unemployed, Underemployed, and Unhappily Employed by Rebecca Anthony and Gerald Roe. Adams Media Corp 1990.

Never Eat Alone, by Keith Ferrazzi. Currency 2005. Never Eat alone:

"The dynamics of status are the same whether you're working at a corporation or attending a society event—"invisibility" is a fat worse than failure."

Guts, Jackie and Kevin Frieberg. Currency 2004.

Life Resume: A life guide to Women over 40, but not over the hill, by Lyn M. Hutchins. Paradox Press 1994.

Manage Your Own Career: Make it a SNAPP by Donald J. Hanratty, Ron Biagi and Tresa Eyres. It's How Publishing Co. 2002.

You Don't Have To Take it! by Ginny Nicarthy. Seal Press 1993. "Is it you? Are you really just too sensitive to harsh words on the job? Or is it abuse? The authors share personal experiences and walk you through defining the problem [on the job], developing a remedy and placing this type of abuse into the larger social context. The workbook format allows you to objectively view your situation and to take appropriate action. Stop feeling powerless; stop feeling as if there must be something wrong with you."

Over 40 Job Search Guide: 10 Strategies for Making Your Age an Advantage in Your Career, by Gail Geary. JIST Works 2004. "A treasure chest that is packed with tips, samples of resumes, interview responses, and real-world examples."

Glossary of Unusual Terms

Alpha and Omega—this is a Judeo-Christian term that literally translates to "first and last." However, I use it to mean "all that there is and ever could be."

BS—nonsense; anything that wastes precious time; crap; bull--it

Celestial Splendor—Heaven

Colored People—People of African Descent

Dem Neck bruck—In Antiguan dialect, in referring to breasts, it means saggy breasts

Diddle squat—nothing; zero

Divine Creation of Interconnectivity—a mysterious, magical thing that connects every human being to each other

Doo doo—big trouble; excrement

E—in Antiguan dialect, it means "He" or "him"

E-Harmony—an online dating site

Empty Wallet Syndrome—a strange affliction that compels a sufferer to spend every dime in their wallets, often mindlessly

Everests—Big goals and ambitions; something that is difficult or seemingly impossible to achieve

Fait accompli—a thing that is accomplished; a thing which is done

Federal State of Emergency aka my life—a life which may require drastic action in order to restore order, peace and productivity

Financial Dire Straits—serious financial delinquency; serious financial problems and hardships

Fourteenth Arrondissement—an area of Paris within close proximity to the Sorbonne.

Frenemy—someone who is not a full fledged enemy and not a full fledged friend.

Frog—the wrong guy or girl (but with a mean streak)

Gee-al—In Antiguan dialect, it means "girl"

Give a fig—care about something or someone. Give a damn.

Good soil—good things, good beginnings, good intentions, smart and intelligent choices; something that makes sense as opposed to something bad or something that does not make sense

Granny Panties—really hideous underwear that is big, roomy and reaches the belly button; atrocious underwear that could reach the rib cage of the wearer; tattered panties.

Herd—the masses; everybody else *en masse*

IS-God

Jump on Oprah's Couch—crazy happiness; being deliriously filled up with joy; a person who is marked for public flogging for expressing exhilarating love for another person (esp. rich and famous persons) i.e. "he's a jump on Oprah's Couch"

Lang—In Antiguan dialect, it means "long"

Latte Factor—how much you spend mindlessly on small things, like Espresso that can really add up to a big expense

M.O.—pattern and style of operating

Mass Card—in the Catholic Church, a card bought by a parishioner to have a mass dedicated to the memory of, or on behalf of someone else.

Match.com—an online dating site

Mek—In Antiguan dialect that means "make"

Min—In Antiguan dialect it often means "had" or "was"

Mongoose—a devious, calculating, smooth operating man who is up to no good and will prey on an unsuspecting girl; a "scavenger"; a "frog"

Mouma—In Antiguan dialect it means "mother"

Navel Knockers—In Antiguan dialect it means "granny panty"

Pannies—Panty

Picknie—In Antiguan Dialect it means "child"

Put a pacifier into their mouths—help them

Quid pro quo—this for that; tit for tat

Reproductive Endocrinologist—a doctor who specializes in infertility and other hormonal and gynecological issues pertaining to a woman's reproductive issues; a doctor who assists a woman with her "rendezvous with a turkey baster."

Schmucks—s.o.b.s; people who are either not nice, or who are not "winners;" idiots

Sisyphus—(from Wikipedia) a king punished in the Tartarus by being cursed to roll a huge boulder up a hill, only to watch it roll down again, and repeat this throughout eternity.

Tek—In Antiguan dialect it means "take"

The Invisible—God, or some supernatural thing or force

U—In Antiguan dialect it means "you"

Vajayay—Vagina (slang)

Wa—In Antiguan dialect it means "what"

Wrongheaded—a mistake in judgment

Index

4

40 Wall, 43, 235
401K, 45, 46

A

Abundance, 37, 38, 54, 55, 56, 77, 84, 106, 181, 186, 255, 258, 261, 278
Academy Award, 28
Addictions, 63, 66
Adolescence, 67, 198
Africa, 65, 199
Alexander Graham bell, 214
Alpha and the Omega, 31, 254
Amarillo, Texas, 205
America, 30, 165, 199, 204, 236
American Idol, 64, 234
Amtrak, 19
Andre Oprah's hairdresser, 73
Angelina Jolie, 73
Annulment., 140
Antigua, 96, 122
Apple, 46
Apprentice, 94, 105, 129, 187, 191, 219, 239, 258
Asian Countries, 186
Asprey, 58, 94
Atlanta, Georgia, 19
Atlantic City, 57

B

Bahamas, 96
Bankrupt, 60, 61, 165, 187, 261
Baptists, 88
Barbara Walters, 169
Barron Trump, 93
Beautiful woman, 66, 141, 161
Beauty, 73, 74, 94, 131, 173, 207, 271
Beef Ranchers, 205
Ben Affleck, 28
Bergdorf Goodman., 58
Best friend Gayle (Oprah's), 72
Best Screen Play, 28
Beyonce Knowles, 132
Bible, 30, 67
Big shots, 143
Bill Gates, 34, 214
Billion dollar business, 75, 86, 257
Biological Child, 123
Bishops and Popes and Cardinals, 54
BMWs, 30
Breast Lift, 122, 131
Brioni Suits, 50
British, 220
Britney Spears, 80, 86, 162, 260
Broadway, 64, 79, 264, 268
Brooklyn, 86, 133, 176, 188
Buddhist, 88
Bull in the china closet., 69
Bullies, 172, 174, 260

Butt, 62, 103, 121, 131, 137

C

Cake, 223, 249
California, 25, 167
Capricorn, 21, 193
Caribbean, 53, 138
Carolyn Kepcher, 112
Carrie Bradshaw, 45
Catholic, 53, 88, 283
Catholics, 54
Celebrity Apprentice, 129
Cellulite, 138, 140, 141
Central Park, 85, 111
Champs Elysees, 225
Character flaw, 64
Chartres, 225
Chicago, 24, 150, 167, 227, 228
Childhood, 65, 198
Childish Things, 59, 67, 68, 72, 73
Chinchillas, 35
Christ, 31, 277
Churches, 55
Coach potato, 182
Coke habit, 245
Commandments, 99
Competition, 25, 105, 258
Condom, 182
Conscience, 21, 64, 97
Creative genius, 86

D

David Bach, 49, 268
Deity, 53
Demi Moore, 159
Democracy, 109
Democratic Primaries, 238
Denzel Washington, 73
Depression, 64, 97
Desires, 41, 62, 76, 165, 277
Diana Ross, 24, 72
Diane Sawyer, 72
Divine creation of interconnectivity, 109
DIVORCE, 141
DNA, 33
Domestic Diva, 94
Donald Trump, 23, 24, 25, 30, 34, 37, 42, 49, 50, 52, 57, 60, 63, 65, 66, 72, 73, 79, 80, 84, 85, 92, 93, 99, 103, 104, 111, 118, 122, 124, 128, 135, 140, 146, 150, 155, 161, 167, 168, 169, 170, 172, 177, 179, 181, 185, 187, 190, 195, 201, 206, 207, 211, 216, 221, 227, 230, 232, 235, 236, 237, 241, 242, 247, 251, 252, 254, 267, 269, 280
Dr. Phil, 73
Drugs, 66, 182, 183, 185, 246
Duane Reade, 58
Dubai, 25

E

Earth, 33, 34, 50, 62, 66, 80, 222
E-Harmony, 127, 281
Elders, 54
Empty Wallet Syndrome, 52, 281
Estate Planning, 47
Europe, 60
Euros, 224
Eve, 125, 141
Everest, 223, 229
Exotic fruits, 35

F

Fashionistas, 35
Fat, 141, 172, 173, 279
Federal-state-of-emergency, 41
Fico Score, 61
Fifth Avenue, 57
First Lady., 204
Flesh, 35, 136, 238, 259
Fortieth birthday, 82, 165
Fourteenth Arrondissement, 224, 282
Frenemy, 156
Friend, 72, 73, 79, 93, 105, 148, 149, 150, 151, 152, 153, 155, 167, 173, 209, 244, 251, 260, 282

G

Garden of Eden, 125
Generational Trusts, 47
Genetic Code, 53
Gentile, 88
George Clooney, 73, 94, 173
Georgia, 19
Georgia Peach, 60
Ghettos of Milwaukee, 24
God, 19, 25, 31, 32, 33, 34, 35, 37, 38, 39, 40, 41, 53, 55, 62, 79, 81, 88, 89, 99, 105, 118, 125, 126, 133, 137, 145, 162, 179, 195, 199, 200, 201, 216, 217, 218, 231, 238, 242, 248, 252, 255, 262, 277, 283, 284
Golden Girls, 203
Granny Panties, 126
Gratitude journal, 80, 120
Gray hairs, 137
Greyhound Buses, 122
Greys Anatomy, 234
Gwyneth Paltrow, 120

GYN, 176, 178

H

Half full, 213, 215, 216, 217, 262
Halle Berry, 133, 159, 219
Hamptons, 83, 97, 144
Happiness, 64, 97, 127, 133, 153, 243, 244, 245, 246, 247, 283
Harry Winston, 58
Hawaii, 138, 167
Health, 77, 97, 109, 122, 132, 180, 181, 182, 183, 184, 185, 186, 261, 265, 274, 277
Heaven, 53, 54, 62, 80, 86, 125, 176, 242, 250, 281
Heavens, 43
Heirlooms., 58
Herd, 234, 235, 236, 237
Hillary Clinton, 73, 81, 107, 222
History, 40
Hollywood, 131, 161, 204
Honey, 35
Hormones, 218
Hurricane, 199

I

Investment Bank, 34
Iowa Caucus, 81, 238
Ivana Trump, 85, 125
Ivanka Trump, 43, 74, 162, 169

J

Janice Dickson, 131
Jennifer Anniston, 73, 191, 203, 204

Jesus, 24, 25, 30, 37, 38, 42, 43, 49, 50, 54, 57, 58, 60, 65, 66, 67, 72, 75, 79, 80, 85, 86, 92, 95, 96, 99, 103, 104, 105, 111, 112, 118, 124, 125, 128, 129, 135, 136, 140, 141, 146, 150, 151, 155, 156, 161, 162, 167, 168, 172, 174, 179, 185, 186, 190, 191, 195, 201, 202, 206, 207, 208, 211, 216, 221, 222, 227, 228, 232, 233, 236, 237, 241, 242, 247, 248, 251, 252, 254, 277
Jewish, 88
Jimmy Choo, 35, 164, 166
Jimmy Choos, 83, 163, 164, 167, 194
Joan Collins, 70
Joan Rivers, 131
John Travolta, 72
Jump on Oprah's couch, 248, 263
Juvenile bundle of nerves, 68

K

Kanye West, 132
Kathy Lee Gifford, 131
Katie Holmes, 245
Korean Deli, 58
Kosciusko Mississippi, 24

L

Labor Day, 161
Late-Bloomer, 41
Latte Factor, 49, 283
Law Guardian, 220
Lindsay Lohan, 87
Live your best life, 27, 30, 42, 66, 72, 85, 99, 104, 118, 161, 190, 195, 221, 251
Louvre Museum, 225
Luxemburg Gardens (Paris), 225

M

M.O., 105, 283
Mac mansion, 19
Macy's, 50
Madison Avenue, 58
Manhattan, 43, 45, 85, 235
Manolo Blaniks, 45, 83
Maria Shriver, 73
Marla Maples Trump, 60, 125
Married Man, 60, 61
Martha Stewart, 83
Martin Luther King, 214
Mass Card, 133, 283
Match.com, 127, 283
Maya Angelou, 73
Mega Lotto, 233
Melania Trump, 25, 58, 74, 93, 125
Meltdowns, 69
Meredith Vieira, 169
Michael Bloomberg, 107
Michael Jackson, 108, 131
Microsoft, 46
Middle East, 34
Midtown Manhattan, 86
Military school, 237
Mink, 35
Mistakes, 60, 66, 128, 256
Modeling agency, 74
Money, 25, 35, 46, 47, 49, 50, 51, 52, 53, 54, 55, 58, 61, 74, 86, 94, 111, 122, 135, 156, 158, 164, 165, 171, 185, 186, 187, 188, 189, 191, 224, 225, 226, 244, 255, 256, 261, 270, 276, 278
Mongoose, The, 142
Mother Nature, 131
Movie star, 245
Movie stars, 138

Mr. Big, 45
Mr. Right, 115
Mr. Trump, 20, 30, 95, 129, 154, 157, 169, 230, 231, 257, 260
Mr. Wrong, 116, 224
Mud bath, 169
Mudslinging, 169, 170

N

Nag, 197, 198, 201, 202, 262
Nannies, 57
National Geographic, 238
Nelson Mandela, 73
New Hampshire primary, 218, 219
New York, 23, 80, 82, 85, 93, 97, 111, 143, 156, 199, 226, 227, 228, 232, 235, 242, 275
New York Politics, 93
New York Real Estate, 85
New York Times Best-Selling Book, 97
Nicole Kidman, 131, 159
Nicolette Sheridan, 159
NY, 25
NYC, 19, 43, 57

O

Off Shore-Trusts, 96
Old Country, 127
Old Testament, 67
Omarosa, 129, 219
Oprah Shows, 49
Oprah Winfrey, 52, 73, 97, 104, 118
Oprah., 20, 27, 245
Oscar, 219
out Melania on top of the piano, 74

Oval Office, 107
OWN, 42, 79

P

Palm Beach., 228
Pam Anderson, 159
Pamela Anderson, 131, 133
Paris Hilton, 46, 162, 219
Paris, France, 46, 80, 87, 143, 223, 224, 225, 226, 227, 228, 282
Park Avenue Law Firm, 187
Pastors, 54
Penis, 123, 150
Penn Station, 19
Pennies, 52, 53, 56
Perfect Beauty, 56
Personal Secretaries, 58
Philosophers, 76
Philosophy, 40, 165, 269
Pirate, 33
Plastic surgery, 183
Plastic Surgery, 131, 132, 135
Plaza Hotel, 85
Politicians, 45, 199
Posh Spice, 131
Poverty, 32, 54
Prada, 20
Prenup, 94, 195
President, 40, 107, 204, 238
President Bill Clinton, 40, 238
Prey, 142, 145, 146, 284
Priceless commodities., 34
Private chef, 140
Private hairdresser, 83
Private Jets, 20, 23, 24
Profanity, 63

Provence, 225

Q

Queens, 86, 124
Quincy Jones, 72

R

Rabbis, 54
Rainbow, 240
Regrets, 65
Religious fanatic, 40
Rhonda Byrne, 197, 269
Rich, 32, 33, 34, 35, 36, 37, 39, 40, 41, 45, 53, 54, 55, 136, 164, 170, 181, 186, 203, 246, 259, 267, 268, 269, 283
Romeo, 116
Rosie O'Donnell, 169
Roth IRA, 47
Royalty, 94, 144
Rubrics cube, 209, 210, 211

S

Sarah Jessica Parker, 83
Scientists, 39, 40
Secrets of a Millionaire Mind, 203
Sex, 127, 141, 182, 183, 259
Sexual Development, 68
Sexual energy, 70
Sexy, 45, 70, 114, 126, 138, 163, 164
Sidney Poitier, 72
Slovenia, 25
Soccer mom, 105, 258

South Africa, 65, 167, 205
Spiritual Life, 116
Star Jones, 132, 170, 173
Steadman Graham, 79, 92, 128, 140, 150
Steroids, 109, 183
Steve Wynn, 105
Supermodels, 128
Supremes, 24
SUV, 68
Suze Orman, 49, 268
Switzerland, 96
Synagogues, 55

T

T Harv Eker, 203, 270
Taxes, 96
Telescopes, 39
Temper tantrums, 69
The Invisible, 29, 284
The Oprah Winfrey Academy for Girls., 65
The Science of Getting Rich, 32
The Secret,, 197, 269
The View, 173
Think Big and Kick Ass, 186
Think Big and Kick Ass, 99, 206, 267
Think like a Billionaire, 52, 74
Tina Turner, 73
Today Show, 169
Tom Cruise, 73, 245
Traditional IRA, 47
Trans fats, 32, 182
Treachery., 61, 142
Trump, 23, 25, 30, 34, 37, 42, 49, 50, 52, 57, 60, 63, 65, 66, 72, 73, 75, 79, 80, 84, 85, 92, 93, 99, 103, 104, 111, 118, 122, 124, 128, 135, 140, 146, 150, 155, 161, 167, 169, 172, 177, 179, 181, 185, 187, 190, 195, 201,

206, 207, 211, 216, 221, 227, 230, 231, 232, 235, 236, 237, 241, 247, 251, 257, 267, 269
Trump Tower, 25, 57, 227
Tuileries Gardens (Paris), 225
TV Network, 42
Tyra Banks, 159

U

United Emirates, 43, 228
United Nations Ambassador, 204
Universe, 39, 74, 77, 173, 253, 259
Upstate New York, 83

V

Valentino, 20

Vegas, 25, 105
Vermin, 94
Victoria's Secret, 127
Vodka, 105

W

Wall Street, 80, 143
Weakling, 238, 240
Wharton, 74, 162, 237
White House, 97, 107
Wikipedia, 197, 284

Y

Yacht, 60

www.ingramcontent.com/pod-product-compliance
Lightning Source LLC
Chambersburg PA
CBHW080432110426
42743CB00016B/3141